BELGO
COOKBOOK

BELGO
COOKBOOK

DENIS BLAIS
AND ANDRÉ PLISNIER

Clarkson Potter/Publishers
New York

CONTENTS

FOREWORD

by MICHAEL JACKSON

L ET US GET the wine-and-food question out of the way first. Where would you most readily find an impeccably selected list of fine French wines, and cuisine to match? In Brussels. No city has as many fine restaurants per head of population. Why is this so little known? Because the Belgians don't talk much about food: They demand the best, usually get it, and know it when they see it. Most often, they enjoy it with beer.

This is not always obvious. That flûte on the table: Surely it contains pink Champagne? You saw a Champagne bottle being uncorked? Well, no: The bottle contained a winey-tasting aperitif, Framboise – a Lambic beer tinged with raspberries. The Burgundy sampler, full of a darker red liquid? That is Rodenbach, an oak-aged beer to cut the richest cassoulet. And that brandy snifter? It embraces the aromas of a rich, chocolatey digestif beer from a Trappist monastery.

A Belgian Trappist monk, who apparently has his own code of denial, once insisted that I try his beer with asparagus. In Belgium, lovers of that seasonal speciality are also inclined to dine off hop shoots prepared in much the same way. Fortunately, they leave sufficient hops to spice their beer.

Beer to arouse the appetite for a meal that will be delicate in flavors but hearty in portion. Beer as an ingredient in the dish – not just in steamed mussels or carbonade flamande, but in countless other dishes – even in desserts. Beer as an accompaniment and as a digestif. There is a sense of relish here that can be recognized in the paintings of Bruegel, where beer

and food are served with a generosity to tempt the gods. The sensuous land of Rubens, the surrealistic *terroir* of Magritte, has a rich creativity.

I once spoke at a dinner in New York prepared by four Belgian chefs, boasting between them six Michelin stars. Most of the dishes were prepared with beer, and we had a different brew with each course. The Belgians call this *cuisine à la bière*. It is not the whole story of their kitchen, any more than moules and frites are (though that is surely one of the world's classically simple meals, especially with a glass of the beer called Gueuze).

For years, I have spoken and written about the joys of Belgian beer and food, but Denis and André have made this wonderful combination available in the USA. Now, they have a word of subversive advice: *Do* try this at home.

DO TRY THIS AT HOME.

Michael Jackson, presenter of The Beer Hunter, *is author of* The Beer Companion *and* The Great Beers of Belgium, *and winner of the Mercurius Award, presented by Crown Prince Philippe of Belgium.*

7

THE Belgo
EXPERIENCE..

I N 1986 — when Belgium managed to make it past the Soccer World Cup quarter finals by defeating the Soviet Union — we were probably the only two guys in London waving the Belgian flag who didn't work at the Embassy. Lonesomely celebrating this historic Belgian victory, we set our minds on finding a restaurant that would serve a large casserole of *moules* with crispy *frites* and lashings of mayonnaise. We had to settle for a lukewarm pint of Stella Artois and a bag of soggy French fries. That night we made a promise to bring the moules-frites-bières experience to London.

We spent the next six years trying to convince banks and investors that London was in great need of a Belgian restaurant serving unpretentious traditional food. With the heydays of the Eighties long dead, a major recession, and London restaurants going bust every five minutes, we had our work cut out. Our biggest obstacle was investment. But our second one was Belgium: People simply laughed at us. Belgium's image in Britain was hardly as fashionable as Italy, Spain, or California, and potential investors were very skeptical about mussels being the main feature on our menu. "The English will not eat mussels," they said. Sorry chaps — you were wrong!

It took the consumption of a few more stale Stellas before Belgo opened it's doors to the north London public in April 1992. Eighteen months later we had to double the seating capacity. In April 1995 we opened the 400-seat beer hall and restaurant Belgo Centraal in Covent Garden. In January 1998

the company was floated on the stock market and went through a period of rapid expansion, opening restaurants in New York City, Dublin, and two more in London, including a new Belgo concept called Bierodrome, dedicating most of its attention to the beers and genevers of Belgium.

Designing and packaging the Belgo concept was a real challenge, taking into consideration the Belgian image problem and general lack of interest. We love Belgium's food and all it's quirkiness .We love the jokes and we love the beers. For us that's all we needed to be convinced that Belgo would work. And besides, the British always love an underdog.

Belgium's historical culinary and cultural background played a major role in preparing the "briefs" for the design teams of both of the original Belgo restaurants in London. The first Belgo, a monastic refectory with wooden brewery-style tables and staff in Trappist monk-like habits, was inspired by Belgium's strong brewing tradition and the simplicity of the food. The high-tech feel was attributed to the fact that, although Belgium is deeply rooted in it's traditional past, it now plays a very important role in the artistic and political landscaping of Europe. Anand Zenz, who was responsible for Belgo Noord, was highly successful in his eccentric interpretation of the European brewery eating hall, designing pick-axe-handled tables and chairs, and a mechanomorphic kitchen air-extraction system. The concrete rendered walls and facade are there to remind us of the concrete sea barricades from Oostende to Blankenberge. The striking and

Belgo
NOORD

Belgo
CENTRAAL

often comical lettering embedded into the restaurant walls are medieval names for common fare, mainly fish, from Rabelais' *Pantagruel* and *Gargantua*, such as Donkeythistle, Tumturdy, and Thornback. This was a rather ingenious way to avoid having to hang tiresome Brueghel and Magritte reproductions on the walls. It also gave the restaurant a certain peasantish and festive atmosphere.

Belgo Noord's later extension, designed by the world renowned Ron Arad, experimented with external forms and interior space. The result was to reinvent the Biergarten concept with acid-etched steel and plywood beams soaring in and out of a glass roof, mirror-finish table tops, and a dyed-concrete base bar complete with an amoeba-shaped wooden top.

Back in Covent Garden, in the center of London, the 12,000 square feet of Belgo Centraal provided the sheer size that the Belgo concept has always deserved. Work on the site began in November 1994 and Ron Arad and Associates were commissioned to create a Belgo themed on Belgium's central geographical position in Europe, incorporating high volume transit and, of course, the brewing trade. The result here was of sheer industrious, machine-like, wonder.

And when Belgo arrived on American shores, the sleek design of its European sisters was not left behind. Answering the American diners' burgeoning interest in Belgian cuisine, Belgo also presents them with a striking space designed by Spanish architect Alejandro Zaera-Polo. Walking past the open kitchen and along Belgo Nieuw York's long ramps, diners enter the main dining hall — where a towering vaulted ceiling evokes a velodrome, or cycling hall. Combining sophistication with beer hall tradition, New Yorkers can enjoy eating their moules side by side at

communal wooden tables or while nestling at one of Belgo's stylish banquettes.

The six years spent preparing the Belgo "package" were not used up focusing solely on the design and architectural aspects of the projects. As a matter of fact, 70% of our time was concentrated on researching the food and drink of Belgium: The heart and soul of Belgo. André, being Belgian, was brought up with delights such as *moules et frites* and *waterzooi de poulet,* and for him it was a childhood dream to have a restaurant that would feature all his family's favorite recipes. Denis, having lived for five years on the Continent, mainly in Cologne, was desperate to have a brewery-style restaurant that served unpretentious and inexpensive food with superb quality beers. Belgium was calling!

Much to our delight, Belgo was an instant success.

A traditional Belgian cuisine cookbook was definitely needed in the English language. So, when the offer came to do this book, we felt we not only had the golden opportunity to assemble all the delicious recipes of Belgo's favorite dishes, but also the challenge to make a cookbook exciting. Our apologies go to all the cookbook fans out there, but we always felt that, for average Joes like us, cookbooks were nice to look at but unusable or incomprehensible. We hope we've changed that with this book by creating a guide to the strange world of day-to-day Belgo-isms and easy-to-use recipes using simple accessible ingredients.

The *Belgo Cookbook* is a compilation of the best-loved dishes we have served in Belgo. It includes all the Belgian traditional favorites such as *waterzooi de poulet* and *carbonnades flammandes* but the main accent is on the *cuisine à la bière* and *moules et frites*, the true national dish

Moules &

\+

Frites & Bière

10,000 TONS OF MUSSELS LATER...

of Belgium. Oh yes, we have even included our secret recipe for our French fries.

We have tried to keep the layout of this book similar to our menus. In true Belgo fashion we made sure the design would be as you've never seen before — and yet familiar and user-friendly, making it easy to follow, especially to the Belgo fanatics that we see week after week, year in, year out.

You should have no trouble finding any of the raw ingredients recommended in our recipes. Items such as celery root (celeriac) can now be found in good supermarkets. Special potatoes, like the Bintjes, mentioned on page 42, can also be ordered from good food merchants.

All the Belgian beers and genevers in this book can be purchased directly from Belgo. Cooking with beer may seem unusual to some — especially with fish — but it is a method that has been used for centuries in Flanders and Wallonia with tasty results. We have tended to laugh when some of the British press has referred to Belgo's food as fashionable or even trendy. Belgium fashionable in New York? (No wonder poor old King Beaudoin passed away. He could finally rest in peace.) The food has been fashionable in Belgium for

hundreds of years— we merely wanted to celebrate it with a wider audience. Belgian fare is for people who want to eat it, not philosophically dissect it. We hope this book helps you make a Belgian celebration, feast, or simple snack an everyday joy.

So, 10,000 tons of mussels later, what is the question we most often get asked?

Q. *HOW DO YOU STILL MANAGE TO EAT MUSSELS AFTER SEEING SO MANY EVERY DAY?*

A. *WITH FRITES AND MAYO!*

(BOYS
& GIRLS,
LET'S GO)

ALLEZ PEI ET MEI

Denis & André

Moules,
Muscheln, Mosselen, Cozze, Mussels!

LOOKING FOR A FEW QUARTS of high quality, clean mussels is one thing: Looking for 1 ton per day is another. At Belgo we cook up to 7 tons of fresh mussels per week. Part of those six years doing preparational research was spent looking into this slightly intimidating task. But with all honesty, we pessimistically anticipated selling only some 1-2 tons per week, which goes to show how suprised we were with Belgo's phenomenal success.

THEY WERE WRONG!

CHERCHER LA MOULE

DURING OUR INTREPID RESEARCH, part of our problem was to assure year-round supplies. So sourcing batches of mussels that were not spawning, or reproducing, in the mid-May through to July period turned our search into a globe-trotting event. As a result, Belgo in London has served fresh mussels from Canada, Denmark, Holland, Ireland, Scotland, Wales and, yes, even England. In North America, mussels are easily available from the coast of Maine and Prince Edward Island. In winter months there are rope-grown mussels that are harvested through the ice around Newfoundland. In our British restaurants, we use mainly Scottish rope-grown mussels that are cultivated in some of the purest waters in all of Europe, namely Ulg on the west coast of the Isle of Lewis.

Fresh, clean, and well-sheltered waters are absolutely crucial for producing sweet-tasting fleshy mussels. The slightest variation in the degrees of water purity and salinity could have a huge impact on the actual taste of a mussel. After many years of scouring the sea beds, Belgo believes it has found a paradise for rope-grown mussels on Loch Roag and Loch Drovinish, both in Scotland.

"Jock" Mackenzie, founder of Hebridean Seafoods, purchased the 10,000 acres of Saliscro Estate back in 1967. After several unsuccessful attempts, "Jock," his son Cree, and production manager, Peter Macleod, got to grips with the usual engineering difficulties that arise from suspended *mytili* culture, and eventually realized the benefits of mussel farming, over the obviously more popular Scottish salmon farming. Belgo quotes Jock's views on the beneficial differences between the two aquacultures: "Mussels feed themselves and come in their own packaging." How true! Mussels are basically "filter feeders," surviving on *phytoplanktons* and tons of organic detritus that are in abundance in Loch Roag and therefore cost-effectively feed themselves.

Thanks to "Jock," Cree, Peter, and numerous other small Scottish mussel farms, Belgo boasts using up to a quarter of all Scottish rope-grown mussels during the season.

So, which country produces the best mussel? Size and taste will vary in different waters and most producers will wave their own flag. The French like the smallish tasty Bouchot mussel, which is cultivated on long poles or stakes driven into shallow water pools or estuaries. Irish mussels, although quite small, have a superb smoky/salty taste. Check out the Bantry Bay mussel festival in mid-May on the south-coast and while you're down there say hello to John Murphy of Fastnet Mussels. The Dutch and the Belgians will pay outrageous prices for their large "Goulden" mussels that are mainly grown on state-distributed mussel beds on the bottom of the world's most famous mussel-growing pools, the Escaut, off the shores of Yerseke in Holland. Koe Prins, the mussel producer "king," claims his outfit, Prins and Dingemans, can produce up to 50,000 tons per day. Maybe…but Jan of Anderssens in Agessund, Denmark, can dredge up to 100,000 tons of the super-large, wild Danish mussels that grow on the world's largest natural mussel farm,

MUSSELS FEED THEMSELVES AND COME IN THEIR OWN PACKAGING

the Limfjord. Having said that, most of Denmark's delicious mussels are used for processing: in cans, jars, and frozen. And guess who owns most of Anderssens? You got it: The Dutch mussel "king" himself. The Scots have supplied Belgo year-round because of the quality and freshness of their produce, so hats off to Jock Mackenie and co.

So is bigger better? A good-sized mussel will have up to 28-30% mussel meat weight content and usually takes up to two years to grow. At Belgo we use different sizes for different serving styles. In our 4-quart mussel pots we will use an average minimum meat weight size of 28%. Our mussel platters require a larger-sized mussel of at least 30% and that's because they are first blanched or cooked just enough to open before grilling. Hence the larger meat content remains substantial when serving the dish. These large "Jumbo" mussels can take three to four years to grow and can reach up to 45% meat weight content. Belgo recommends the medium-size mussel simply because the mussel texture and taste is at it's best in the early parts of its second year. At that age they are known as spats or juvenile mussels.

Wild mussels can spawn from May to September and are collected or they settle on long ropes that hang down from flotation rafts. The best time to collect spats is from mid-April to mid-July. They cling onto these long polypropylene ropes for the rest of their sweet, dear lives. These little spats need a great deal of expert attention. Routine check-ups on them include stock density, water temperature, and removal of marine fouling such as seasquirts and seastars. The greatest threat is the infamous "red tide," a discoloration caused by algae that raises the toxicity in the water, thus cutting off the mussels' oxygen and making the crustacean dangerously poisonous. But have no fear! First, the mussels sort themselves out once the red tide passes by filtering themselves. Second, all farmed mussels are cultivated in strictly monitored waters. Any signs of toxicity in the water will be identified immediately and all farmers will be subsequently forbidden to continue cultivation. All mussels should be grown in Grade A waters. If they are not they will need fresh sea-water purification treatment before they are sold at market.

GET RID OF THAT BEARD!

How do these large, fresh-mussel producers manage to de-beard, or de-biste as it's more commonly known in the trade, the tons of mussels that are on demand daily? Huge conveyor belt-like channels, pumped with chilled sea water, drive and rinse the just-landed "grapes" of mussels before they are re-directed onto another belt with small permeated stainless-steel rollers that continuously roll in opposite directions, catching the mussel beard and tearing it off. *Ouch* times 10 tons. The mussels are then dropped onto sorting machines which shake the freshly "shaved" mussels onto a bed of pipes with gaps in between them that vary in size. The mussels eventually find their own way into their appropriate basket size and await bagging and tagging. Tag names vary according to size: Extras, Supers, Imperials, Jumbos, Goldens.

Q. WHAT DO YOU CALL A BABY MUSSEL?

A. A BRUSSEL!

Here are Denis and André's
MUSSEL TIPS AND MYTHS:

1 Smell the mussels you are about to buy. Look out for any that are gasping and have an overly strong, pungent fishy smell. A fresh bag of mussels will smell of the sea and nothing else.

2 Rope-grown mussels have thinner body meat and tend to be sweeter in taste. Because their shells tend to be thinner, you might find more crushed or dead mussels, which you should discard. Rope-grown mussels require less cleaning time and should be totally grit free.

3 Bottom-cultured or dredged mussels are usually purified in large holding tanks. During that process all impurities, sand, or grit should be removed. If they have clean shells it means that they have been through this process. If you are buying local mussels and they seem very dirty, make sure you give them a good rinse under very cold water (seawater if available). Do not let them sit in a sink full of fresh water as this will eventually drown them.

4 Remove the mussel beards by pinching and pulling. Do not remove the beards unless you plan to cook the mussels immediately. De-bearding lowers the mussels' shelf life. Mussels may have up to five days of shelf life if they are stored under the correct conditions.

5 If a mussel opens up before you cook it, tap it on a hard surface. It should close itself . If it doesn't, discard it.

6 If a mussel does not open once you've cooked it, do not eat it.

7 Like pasta, mussels can be served with thousands of different sauces. So get your chef's hat on and create.

8 Mussel Art: *Casserole and Closed Mussels*, 1964, by Marcel Broodthaers, in the Tate Gallery, London.

9 Mussels are one of the heathiest food stuffs on earth. They are packed with minerals, high in protein, and very low in saturated fats. They are supposedly the best thing for the common cold.

10 Before hand-picking mussels locally, check with the local Coast Guard for water purity in that area. Hand-picking is not recommended unless you are an expert.

Denis and André's
GUIDE TO COOKING MOULES

1 Cook your mussels in a large, covered pan over high heat. After 1 minute, lift lid to release the first steam.

2 Cover again and continue cooking for 2–3 minutes more. Shake occasionally to stir the mussels.

3 After 3–4 minutes, your mussels should all be open and ready to eat. Discard any unopened mussels.

4 Get your frites and beers ready. Start eating. Allez pei!!!

POTS OF MOULES

A steaming pot of mussels, accompanied by a bowl of freshly made, crisp golden frites, with creamy mayonnaise, is the heart of Belgian food. Every restaurant in Belgium has its own way of cooking mussels—some offer dozens of variations—and we, too, have our favorites.

At Belgo we serve them in a large casserole dish (about 1½ gallons capacity) with a deep lid to collect the empty shells. It holds 2¼ lbs of mussels, which we reckon is just right for one person, but Belgo is famous for its gargantuan helpings. Our mussel platters (pages 33-37), were created for those with less than gargantuan appetites.

To make the final preparation as painless as possible, you can clean the mussels (see page 21) earlier in the day.

VIVE LA MOULE!

Moules à la bière et aux lardons (Mussels with beer and bacon)

2¼ lbs mussels, cleaned
1 small onion, chopped
½ celery stalk, chopped
2 strips smoked bacon, cut into ½-inch squares
½ cup beer (preferably Leffe Blonde)
bouquet garni
beurre manié (2 teaspoons softened butter mashed with 2 teaspoons all-purpose flour until smooth)
salt and pepper

Put the mussels in a casserole dish with the onion, celery, and 7 oz water. Cook over high heat, bring to a boil, and cook until the mussels have opened, stirring frequently to ensure the mussels are evenly cooked. This only takes a few minutes.

Strain the cooking liquid through a fine strainer into a measuring pitcher, leaving behind any grit. Discard any mussels that have not opened. Return the opened mussels, in their shells, to the casserole dish.

To make the sauce, sauté the bacon in an uncovered skillet over very low heat until lightly browned. Drain off any fat, then add the beer, bouquet garni, and ½ cup of the strained mussel liquid. Bring to a boil and whisk in the beurre manié to thicken the sauce slightly. Season to taste, pour over the mussels, bring back to a boil, and serve at once.

VARIATION

(Mussels with Trappist ale)

Omit the bacon and replace the blonde beer with Chimay Rouge.

Moules au vin blanc
(Mussels with white wine)

2¼ lbs mussels, cleaned
1 small onion, chopped
1 celery stalk, chopped
½ cup dry white wine
salt and pepper
1 tablespoon chopped fresh parsley

Clean and check over the mussels very thoroughly. Put them in a casserole dish with the onion, celery, wine, and seasoning. Turn the heat up high, cover with a lid, bring to a boil, and cook until the mussels have opened, stirring frequently to ensure they are evenly cooked. This takes only a few minutes.

Add the parsley and serve at once.

Moules bleue
(Mussels with white wine and Roquefort cheese)

2¼ lbs mussels, cleaned
2 cups dry white wine
½ cup Roquefort cheese

Clean and check over the mussels very thoroughly. Put them in a casserole dish with the wine, put over a high heat, bring to a boil. Cook until the mussels have opened, stirring frequently to ensure they are evenly cooked. This takes only a few minutes.

Meanwhile, cut or crumble the cheese into very small pieces. When the mussels are cooked, add the cheese gradually, stirring until it begins to melt. Serve at once.

Moules marinière
(Mussels with celery, onion, and garlic)

2¼ lbs mussels, cleaned
1 small onion, sliced
1 celery stalk, sliced
1 clove garlic, chopped
2 cups dry white wine
salt and pepper
beurre manié (2 teaspoons softened butter mashed with 2 teaspoons all-purpose flour until smooth)–optional
1 tablespoon chopped fresh parsley

Put the mussels in a casserole dish with the onion, celery, garlic, and wine. Put over high heat, bring to a boil, and cook until the mussels have opened, stirring frequently to ensure the mussels are evenly cooked. This takes only a few minutes.

Strain the cooking liquid into a small saucepan, leaving behind any grit, and discard any mussels that have not opened. Return the opened mussels, in their shells, to the casserole dish.

Bring the mussel liquid to a boil and season to taste. If using, whisk in the beurre manié to make a smooth sauce. Add the parsley and pour over the mussels in the casserole dish. Heat through and serve at once.

VARIATION

(Moules with green peppercorns)

Replace the garlic with 2 tablespoons green peppercorns. In this recipe the sauce needs to be thickened with beurre manié.

Moules moutarde (Mussels with mustard and cream sauce)

2¼ lbs mussels, cleaned
1 small onion, chopped
½ celery stalk, chopped
2 cups dry white wine
2 teaspoons Dijon mustard
1 cup heavy cream
1 egg yolk
salt and pepper
1 teaspoon chopped fresh parsley or tarragon

Put the mussels in a casserole dish and combine with the onion, celery, and wine. Over high heat, bring to a boil, and cook until the mussels have opened, stirring frequently to ensure the mussels are evenly cooked. This takes only a few minutes.

Strain the cooking liquid through a fine strainer into a small saucepan, leaving behind any grit, and discard any mussels that have not opened. Return the opened mussels, in their shells, to the casserole dish.

Mix the mustard, cream, and egg yolk until smooth. Bring the mussel liquid to a boil, then remove from the heat, and immediately whisk in the mustard mixture to make a smooth sauce. Season to taste.

Pour the sauce over the mussels in the casserole dish and heat through gently (do not let the sauce boil or it will separate). Sprinkle with chopped parsley or tarragon and serve at once.

HOW TO EAT MOULES

Retain the shell from the first mussel you eat. You should use this shell as a form of pincher to pluck the rest of your mussels. So please…

NO FORKS AND KNIVES!

BELGO'S TOP 10 TUNES

TO LISTEN TO WHILE COOKING BELGIAN FOOD

1. **ET MOI, ET MOI, ET MOI** –
   Jacques Dutronc
2. **ÇA PLANE POUR MOI** –
   Plastic Bertrand
3. **JE SUIS D'ACCORD** –
   Françoise Hardy
4. **JACKY** –
   Jacques Brel
5. **69 ANNÉE EROTIQUE** –
   Serge Gainsbourg
6. **NATIONAL 7** –
   Honeymoon Killers
7. **CHERRY BLOSSOM** –
   Pepe Ramillo and the Mexican Fiesta
8. **MUSCLE OF LOVE** –
   Alice Cooper
9. **LÀ OU Y A DES FRITES** –
   Georgette Plana
10. **DOMINIQUE** –
    The Singing Nun

Moules poulette (Mussels with mushroom, lemon, and cream sauce)

2¼ lbs mussels, cleaned
2 cups dry white wine
2 tablespoons butter
1 cup mushrooms (preferably oyster mushrooms),
   thinly sliced
1 cup heavy cream
juice of ½ lemon
¼ teaspoon crushed black peppercorns
salt

Clean and check over the mussels very thoroughly. Put them in a casserole dish with the wine and 3½ oz water. Over high heat, bring the mixture to a boil, and cook until the mussels have opened, stirring frequently to ensure they are evenly cooked. This takes only a few minutes.

To make the sauce, melt the butter in a saucepan, add the mushrooms, and sauté until just tender. Add the mushrooms to the mussels and bring to a boil, then stir in the cream, lemon juice, pepper, and salt to taste. Heat through and serve at once.

Moules navigateur
(Mussels with curry cream sauce)

2¼ lbs mussels, cleaned

1¾ cups dry white wine

2 tablespoons butter

1 small onion, chopped

1 small carrot, chopped

¼ cup golden raisins

1 teaspoon curry powder

1 teaspoon tomato paste

1 small apple (preferably Golden Delicious)

5 fl oz heavy cream

Put the mussels in a casserole dish with the wine. Over high heat, bring to a boil, and cook until the mussels have opened, stirring frequently to ensure they are evenly cooked. This takes only a few minutes.

Strain the cooking liquid through a fine strainer into a pitcher, leaving behind any grit, and discard any mussels that have not opened. Return the opened mussels, in their shells, to the casserole dish, cover, and set aside.

Melt the butter in a saucepan, add the onion and carrot, and cook over low heat for 2 minutes or until softened but not browned. Add the golden raisins, curry powder, and tomato paste, and cook, stirring, for 1 minute. Gradually stir in the strained mussel liquid. Peel the apple, cut into wedges, and add to the sauce. Let the sauce simmer gently for 5 minutes, then add the cream.

Pour over the mussels and heat through gently. Serve at once.

Moules congo
(Mussels with coconut cream and lemongrass)

2¼ lbs mussels, cleaned

½ cup dry white wine

½ cup butter

1 lemongrass stalk, very finely chopped

2-3 small green chili peppers, finely chopped

1 1-inch piece of fresh ginger, peeled and finely chopped

1 small onion, very thinly sliced

1 small carrot, very thinly sliced

salt

4 tablespoons coconut cream

4 tablespoons heavy cream

1 teaspoon chopped fresh parsley

Put the mussels in a casserole dish with the wine and ½ cup water, over high heat. Bring to a boil, and cook for a few minutes only, until the mussels have opened, stirring frequently to ensure they are evenly cooked.

Strain the cooking liquid through a fine strainer into a pitcher, leaving behind any grit, and discard any mussels that have not opened. Return the opened mussels, in their shells, to the casserole dish; cover and set aside.

Heat the butter in a saucepan, add the lemongrass, chili peppers, and ginger and cook over low heat for 5 minutes. Add the onion and carrot and cook for a further 5 minutes, until softened but not browned. Add the strained mussel liquid and simmer gently for 30 minutes.

Add a pinch of salt, the coconut cream and heavy cream, and simmer for 10 minutes.

Add the mussels and heat through for 2 minutes, then sprinkle with parsley and serve at once.

Moules provençale (Mussels with tomatoes, herbs, and garlic)

2¼ lbs mussels, cleaned
½ cup dry white wine

PROVENÇALE SAUCE

1 tablespoon olive oil
2 onions, chopped
1 celery stalk, chopped
1 garlic clove, chopped
1 teaspoon chopped fresh basil, plus extra to garnish
bouquet garni
1 tablespoon tomato paste
1 lb ripe plum tomatoes, peeled, chopped, or
    1 14-oz can chopped tomatoes
salt and pepper
1 teaspoon sugar

To make the sauce, heat the olive oil in a large saucepan, add the onions, celery, garlic, basil, and bouquet garni, and cook over low heat for 5 minutes or until softened but not browned.

Mix in the tomato paste and tomatoes, salt, pepper, and sugar, and simmer gently for 30 minutes.

Put the mussels in a casserole dish with the wine, over high heat, and bring to a boil. Cook for a few minutes only, until the mussels have opened, stirring frequently to ensure they are evenly cooked.

Pour off the cooking liquid, discard any mussels that have not opened, and return the opened mussels, in their shells, to the casserole dish.

Pour the hot tomato sauce over the mussels and heat through. Sprinkle with chopped basil and serve at once.

Moules garcia (Mussels with shrooms and tomatoes)

Provençale sauce (see left)
½ cup butter
1 cup wild mushrooms, thinly sliced
¼ teaspoon paprika
pinch of cayenne pepper
2¼ lbs mussels, cleaned
3½ fl oz dry white wine
1 teaspoon chopped fresh parsley

First, make the Provençale sauce and set aside. Melt the butter in a saucepan, add the mushrooms, and sauté for 3–4 minutes or until just tender. Add the paprika and cayenne pepper, then add the Provençale sauce and heat through.

Meanwhile, put the mussels in a casserole dish with the wine and 3½ fl oz water. Put over high heat, bring to a boil, and cook for a few minutes only, until the mussels have opened, stirring frequently to ensure they are evenly cooked.

Pour off the cooking liquid, discard any mussels that have not opened, and return the opened mussels, in their shells, to the casserole dish.

Pour the hot sauce over the mussels and heat through. Sprinkle with parsley and serve at once.

Moules snob
(Mussels with lobster sauce)

Lobster bisque (see right)
2¼ lbs mussels, cleaned
½ cup dry white wine

First make the lobster bisque and keep hot.

Put the mussels in a casserole dish with the wine and 3½ fl oz water. Over high heat, bring the mixture to a boil, and cook for a few minutes only, until the mussels have opened, stirring frequently to ensure they are evenly cooked.

Pour off the cooking liquid, discard any mussels that have not opened, and return the opened mussels, in their shells, to the casserole dish.

Pour the hot lobster bisque over the mussels and serve at once.

Bisque de homard
Lobster bisque with brandy

shells of 2 lobsters
1 onion, roughly chopped
1 carrot, roughly chopped
2 tablespoons butter
¼ cup flour
1 tablespoon tomato paste
1 cup dry white wine
2 tablespoons brandy
bouquet garni
1 cup heavy cream
salt and pepper

Preheat the oven to 400° F.

Using a heavy cleaver, roughly chop the lobster shells, and put in a roasting pan. Roast in the hot oven for 20 minutes, then add the onion and carrot, and roast for a further 20 minutes.

Melt the butter in a large saucepan, and add the roasted lobster shells, onion and carrot, and the flour and tomato paste. Stir well to blend evenly.

Meanwhile, deglaze the roasting pan by adding the white wine and brandy and stirring to loosen the residue in the pan. Add this liquid to the saucepan, together with 7 cups water and the bouquet garni. Bring to a boil, then simmer gently for 1½ hours.

Strain into a clean saucepan, taste, and simmer for a little longer if necessary to concentrate the flavor. Stir in the cream and season to taste.

MOULES PLATTERS

Basic preparation of platters

1 lb 2 oz large mussels, cleaned
2 cups dry white wine

Put the mussels in a casserole dish with the wine, over high heat, and bring to a boil. Cook for a few minutes only, until the mussels have opened, stirring frequently to ensure they are evenly cooked.

Strain the cooking liquid through a fine strainer into a pitcher, leaving behind any grit.

Put the mussels in a large bowl with plenty of ice cubes and cover with cold water to cool them as quickly as possible. Rejecting any mussels that have not opened, or that have broken shells, open each mussel, discarding the empty half shell.

Arrange the mussels on the platter, cover with plastic wrap. Keep in the refrigerator, well away from uncooked meat, poultry, and fish.

Moules escargot (Garlic and herb butter)

1 mussel platter (see left)
7 tablespoons butter
2 garlic cloves, crushed
1 tablespoon chopped fresh parsley
splash of Pernod
salt and pepper
wedge of lemon, to garnish

Cut the butter into small pieces, put in a bowl, and leave at room temperature for 30 minutes.

Add the garlic, parsley, Pernod, and salt and pepper, and mix together, using a fork.

Take the mussel platter from the refrigerator and dot with the flavored butter, then put under a hot broiler for 3 minutes. Garnish with a lemon wedge, and serve at once.

Moules ardennaise
(Ham, chicory, and cheese)

1 mussel platter (see page 33)

1 large or 2 small heads of Belgian endive

¼ cup butter

3 tablespoons sugar

salt and pepper

freshly grated nutmeg

¼ cup dry white wine

3 fl oz heavy cream

2 oz Ardennes ham or prosciutto, cut into very thin strips

½ cup Gruyere and Cheddar cheese, grated

Cut the Belgian endive in half lengthwise, remove the core, and then slice thinly. Melt the butter in a wide saucepan, add the Belgian endive, sugar, salt, pepper, and nutmeg, and cook over low heat for 10 minutes. Add the wine to the Belgian endive and continue cooking until the liquid has reduced by half, then add the cream and ham or prosciutto, and cook for 2 minutes longer.

Take the mussel platter from the refrigerator and spoon the sauce over the mussels. Sprinkle with the cheese, then put under a hot broiler for 3–4 minutes, or until golden brown. Serve at once.

Moules pastis
(Fennel, cream, and Pernod)

1 mussel platter (see page 33)

¼ cup butter

½ fennel bulb, trimmed and finely chopped

½ onion, finely chopped

2 tablespoons Pernod

3 fl oz heavy cream

salt and pepper

½ cup Gruyere and Cheddar cheese, grated

Melt the butter in a saucepan, and add the fennel and onion. Cook over low heat, stirring frequently, for 10 minutes, until the fennel and onion are soft but not browned.

Stir in the Pernod, cream, and salt and pepper, and cook for a further 10 minutes.

Take the mussel platter from the refrigerator and spoon the sauce over the mussels. Sprinkle with the cheese, then put under a hot broiler for 3–4 minutes, or until golden. Serve at once.

Moules pizza
(Tomatoes, herbs, and cheese)

1 mussel platter (see page 33)
1 cup Provençale sauce (see page 30)
½ cup Gruyere and Cheddar cheese, grated
sprigs of basil, roughly torn

Take the mussel platter from the refrigerator and spoon the sauce over the mussels. Sprinkle with the cheese, then put under a hot broiler for 3–4 minutes, or until golden brown. Sprinkle the basil over the platter and serve at once.

Moules poulette
(Mushrooms, lemon, and cream)

1 mussel platter (see page 33)
1½ tablespoons butter
1 cup mushrooms (preferably oyster mushrooms),
    thinly sliced
beurre manié (1 teaspoon softened butter mashed with
    1 teaspoon all-purpose flour until smooth)
¾ cup heavy cream
juice of ¼ lemon
¼ teaspoon crushed black peppercorns
salt
½ cup Gruyere and Cheddar cheese, grated

Prepare the mussel platter, reserving the cooking liquid.
    Melt the butter in a saucepan. Add the mushrooms, and sauté until just tender. Bring the mussel liquid to a boil and whisk in the beurre manié . Stir in the cream, lemon juice, peppercorns, and salt to taste. Take the mussel platter from the refrigerator and spoon the sauce over the mussels until they are generously covered. Sprinkle with the cheese, then put under a hot broiler for 3–4 minutes or until golden brown. Serve at once.

Moules espagnole
(Olive oil and garlic)

1 mussel platter (see page 33)
2 garlic cloves
½ cup olive oil
1 large sprig of thyme
salt and pepper
wedge of lemon, to garnish

Peel the garlic and crush it under the blade of a large knife, then put it in a small bowl. Mix in the olive oil, thyme leaves, and salt and pepper.

Take the mussel platter from the refrigerator and spoon the oil mixture generously over the mussels, making sure they are all covered. Put under a hot broiler for 2 minutes. Serve at once, with a lemon wedge.

Moules meunière
(Pan-fried with lemon and butter)

1 mussel platter (see page 33)
1 lemon
½ cup all-purpose flour
2 tablespoons butter
salt and pepper
1 teaspoon chopped fresh parsley

Take the platter from the refrigerator and remove the mussels from their shells, leaving the shells on the platter.

Cut a wedge of lemon to garnish, then squeeze the juice from the remaining lemon and set aside.

Toss the mussels in the flour to coat them evenly, then shake off any excess.

Melt the butter in a skillet until lightly browned. Add the mussels and sauté for 2–3 minutes, until the mussels are golden brown. Return the mussels to their shells on the platter.

Add the lemon juice, salt and pepper, and parsley to the skillet, and stir to deglaze. Pour the lemon butter over the mussels and serve at once, with the lemon wedge.

Moules po'pei
(Spinach and bacon)

1 mussel platter (see page 33)

¼ lb fresh spinach

salt and pepper

2 tablespoons butter

1 small shallot, chopped

1 garlic clove, chopped

3 fl oz heavy cream

freshly grated nutmeg

½ cup Gruyere and Cheddar cheese, grated

Wash the spinach thoroughly. Bring a large saucepan of water to a boil, add a pinch of salt, and the spinach, and boil for 2 minutes. Drain and run cold water over the spinach for 2 minutes, until it is cold. Squeeze the spinach well to remove as much water as possible.

Melt the butter in a saucepan, add the shallot and garlic, and cook over low heat for 2 minutes. Add the cream, salt, pepper, and nutmeg, and simmer gently for 10 minutes.

Meanwhile, chop the spinach very finely. Add the spinach to the sauce and cook for 2 minutes.

Take the mussel platter from the refrigerator and spoon the sauce over the mussels. Sprinkle with the cheese, then put under a hot broiler for 3–4 minutes or until golden. Serve at once.

FRITES,
FRIETEN, FRITAS,
FRENCH fries!

THE FRENCH, THE ENGLISH, and the Spanish all claim to have not only invented the French fry or frite, but also to having the best-tasting ones. If the future of the European Community was to be decided on the outcome of this most serious debate, the Euro MPs would surely play it safe and do as always: Award the honor to Belgium. But this time not for the usual practicality of avoiding huge jingoistic ego battles by giving the "little neutral country" the medal, but simply because anybody who has ever spent any time in Brussels, or Belgium for that matter, would never second guess this decision.

IS THERE LIFE ON MARS? YOU BET!

BOUFFEUR DES FRITES: THE GREAT DEBATE

WHEN IT COMES TO discussing the *Best Frites in the World Award*, there is more than one country that would like to claim not only the title but also the recognition for creating this great gastronomic delight. The French, the Spanish, and, naturally, the Belgians seem always only too ready to have a heated debate over the subject. The English and Irish would surely want a say, too. But when it comes to being part of the total folklore, ridiculed to the point of being recognized as *"un pays de bouffeur de frites"* (a nation of French fry-eaters), Belgium must take first place at the French fry counter! Indeed, it has even been said that expectant Belgian mothers develop square nipples so that their young may familiarize themselves with eating frites from an early age. Folklore does not get any worse than that.

The Belgians flatly refuse to even debate the issue, having what they feel is the historical proof and technical know-how on producing a nice crisp tasty French fry and not just your average, no offense intended, "oil sponge."

Now, if Hercule Poirot were to investigate he would immediately attract protests for the simple fact that he is Belgian. Well, sort of…we are talking about a fictitious character here. OK, then, so let's use André Plisnier, Belgo's own private investigator: He's the son of a Belgian father and an English mother who spends most her time in Spain and who has a French step-sister in Paris.

LOOKING BACK... A BRIEF HISTORY

Extreme climates, civil and religious warfare, all had a devastating impact on the ever-prosperous Low Countries economy. But more importantly, these had some drastic effects on the agricultural front, thus changing people's eating and drinking habits. It was time to make some sacrifices. In short, poor wheat crops made bread hard to produce and the "easy to grow" potato became a wonder veg. Wine became unaffordable so beer (made from barley) stepped in.

The frying of foods is a technique that is believed to have originated in the Mediterranean countries. Hence it could be that the Spaniards introduced the "frying factor" to the besieged Belgians. But the real spud experts were the Lowlanders. The first-ever recorded recipes using potatoes date back to 1604. They were written by a Belgian named Lancelot de Casteau.

WHERE DID YOU GET THAT *PAPAS RADIX?*

The vegetable in question is of South American origin. It's route to Europe belongs to many different tales from as many countries. As far back as the end of the 16th century the potato was grown within the confines of monasteries in Spain and Italy. But it was not being taken seriously as a food substance. Indeed, it was only when the monks from these monasteries discovered the medicinal benefits from the use of this vegetable that botanists, such as Jules Charles de L'Ecluse, started to pay attention.

Mr. de L'Ecluse (a.k.a. Carolus Clusius) was born in France but studied in Louvain, Ghent, and finally Antwerp, where he published his findings in 1601 on the possibilities the *pomme de terre* offered and its nutritional values.

Carolus used the fertile conditions of Flemish soils to

 **OR**

proceed with potato experimentation. There was, needless to say, a great need for an organic food supplement in northern Europe.

THE DEVELOPMENT OF THE *FRITE*

An historian by the name of Jo Gerard found a manuscript in his family archives that dated back to 1781. It was somewhat strangely entitled *"Curiosités de la table dans les Pays-Bas Belges,"* which roughly translated means "Curious dishes from the Belgian Low Countries." We quote:

"The inhabitants of Namur, Andenne, and Dinant have the habit of frying small fish, which they catch in the Meuse, to improve their diet, especially the poor and needy. But when the frost comes and immobilizes the flow of the river, making fishing far too dangerous, the natives cut wedges of potatoes in the shape of little fish and fry them just like they would do with the fish. If I remember well, this practise dates back over at least one hundred years…"

This appears to be the first recorded document that mentions the frying of potatoes. It could well be that the Spaniards took the idea of *patatas fritas* back home with them when Spanish rule ended in Belgium in the early 18th century. Having been rulers over the Belgians, they may have decided no one would argue their claim of invention or that no one would be as interested as, in fact, we are.

Great Britain and Ireland first imported potatoes from the Low Countries in the mid-18th century and at that time had barely started home production. The frying of foods did not catch on in Great Britain as it did on the Continent, so the British claim to the first fries would seem somewhat weak.

As far as the French are concerned, Antoine Parmentier introduced the *pommes de terre* to France in 1780. They didn't start intensive cultivation there until the mid-19th century, therefore substantially weakening *their* claim.

SO, WHO MADE THE DISCOVERY?

Results for historical claim of invention:

BRITAIN:	**0**
FRANCE:	**0**
SPAIN:	**1**
BELGIUM(LC):	**1**

…AND THE NETHER NETHERLANDS…

So far the Dutch have been kept out of this *frite* investigation primarily because the potato was being cultivated mainly where Belgium is situated today. Also, thousands of rich, well-to-do Flemings with all the *frite* know-how took most of their money and know-how to Amsterdam when fleeing the Spanish Inquisition and Philip the II's reign of terror.

The following joke rather nicely sums up the Belgo-Dutch relationship using the *frite* as common ground:

"If you see a dead man clutching to a *cornet de frites* (packet of fries) you know he's a Belgian. If you see a man nicking that packet of fries off the dead man then you know he's a Dutchman."

THE TASTE CHALLENGE

The British Chip

The SBC (Standard British Chip) usually gets too much salt and the attention to the type of potato is often neglected. The result is often a chip that will rapidly go soggy, oily, and floury. Serving the chip with a dousing of good malt vinegar helps though.

The Belgian Frite

The Belgians go a long way to ensure their *frites* are of top quality. They start by using the Bintjes potato reknowned for it's tartness and richness. It does not turn too floury on frying and holds its firmness perfectly. The size of the Belgian *frite* is also very important. It is said that the perfect Belgian fry should have ½ inch on each side ("Sur chaque cotes") and be 2½ inches long.

The next part of the secret is the most important and is definitely a Belgian invention. In the mid-19th century a certain Mr. Coudelier from Ghent recorded his technique of *"double friture,"* or two-step frying procedure. The first part of frying the freshly cut fry (which has been soaked in unsalted water first) is to blanch or cook just the inside of the potato. The correct size of *frite* should blanche easily at 275°F to 300°F in vegetable oil. One must let the *frites* cool off completely before the second stage of frying, which should be at the much higher heat of 350°F to 360°F, until the *frites* are golden.

Belgian housewives' secrets for perfect *frite* cooking range from using only beef-drippings (which were used when oil was unaffordable) to dipping a small piece of nutmeg or a fresh vanilla pod into the oil to enhance the flavor and aroma. Belgian *frites* are mostly served with mayonnaise but were originally served with pickle (something similar to piccalilli) before the French influence.

The French Frite

The French *frite,* cut very thin, is very pleasant and is at first also quite firm and crispy. But it will, due to its thinness, go limp very quickly. These are also served with mayonnaise if you ask for it. By the way, mayonnaise is a French invention thought to have been conceived at a celebration of the capture of Port-Mahon, capital of Minorca, by the French in 1756. It was originally called Mahonnaise. (There are similar stories of Bayonnaise and Mayennaise: The first after a victory in Bayonne, where ham comes from, the other after the Duke of Mayenne, who also claims to be the inventor. Let the French argue over this one.)

The Spanish Patatas Fritas

This is usually a larger cut *frite*, or even a wedge of potato, and depending on the oil that will be used it can have a wonderful flavor, although *fritas* tend to be a bit on the floury side.

Never ask a Belgian the time when he/she is eating their cornet de frites

"French Fries"?

Many Americans and Canadians fought in Belgium during the great battles of the Second World War. They were totally unfamiliar with the fried potato wedge. As poor old Belgium was struggling to make ends meet through this rather turbulent period in history, the *frites* kept the nation and its saviors/conquerors fed. The *fritkot* or fry wagons everywhere were the most popular restaurants in Belgium and became instant temporary landmarks. And it seems that most were manned by Belgian soldiers, who had to officially speak French, according to the rules of what was left of the Belgian Army. So the fresh faced, not-so-hot on geography Yanks and Canucks were hearing these French-speaking chaps frying up these potato slices and one thing must have led to the other. Hence "French fries." So the legend goes. It's a shame to spoil the story, but the term "French fries" was, in fact, already used in the 19th century.

THE RESULT OF
THE CHIPS-FRITES-FRITAS-FRIETEN TASTE CHALLENGE:
(Points scale 0 to 5, 5 for PERFECT!)

Belgium:	4
Spanish:	1
Britain:	2
France:	3

INSPECTOR BELGO NOTES THAT BELGIUM WINS.

Note that Belgium does not get a perfect score. (So there is such a thing as justice in the French fry Olympics. Watch that judge from Norway with that 4.9 score…) The reason being that, as in most large cities, demand and profit margins put too much pressure on tradition. Hence most of Brussels' *fritures* or *fritkot* will unfortunately use frozen frites. *Fritkots* are ubiquitous, so if you want true Belgian frites one should be careful. It has been said that "there are more chip wagons in Brussels than phone booths!"

So that you don't get a false impression, Belgo will give you a real insider's guide to the best *friture* and *fritkots* of Brussels.

BELGO'S TOP 3 BRUSSELS *FRITURE* & *FRITKOT*

1. La Fritkot à Martin:
This is in front of the beautiful Église de St. Josse on the corner of rues St. Josse and Verbist. Martin inherited this totally unpretentious French fry wagon from his parents and is usually open till 7pm weekdays and later on weekends.

2. La Fritures St. Antoine:
Established in 1948, it is located at Place Jourdan in Etterbeeck. The taxi driver's favorite, this used to be a *kot* but with success came expansion.

3. La Friture de la gare de Uccle:
For your last-minute, late-night snack and a bit of action, check out this old Brussels train stop. Good *frikadellen* (meatballs), too.

Denis and André's

GUIDE TO COOKING FRITES

1 The perfect Belgian frite should be ½ inch on each side and 2½ inches long.

2 Soak freshly cut frites in cold water for 10–15 minutes to wash off starch.

300° F

3 The most important step is the "double friture," which means frying twice: First at 300°F.

350° F

4 Let the frites cool completely before frying for the second time at 350°F.

5 Once your frites are crispy and golden brown, salt lightly, and dip in Belgian mayonnaise to have a real treat. Allez!

BIÈRE,
BIER, BIRRA, CERVEZA, BEER!

IF THE FRENCH BELIEVE that life is merely "something that happens between meals," it could be said that Belgians believe that "beers are the essence of life itself." One of our aims at Belgo was to introduce a beer-drinking culture that would enlighten the public on the wide variety of Belgian beers available and develop interest in their versatility in combination with great food. We felt that good restaurant menus were not promoting beers and that wines were generally getting far too much credit. With over 650 Belgian beers to choose from, we knew Belgo would be able to create a beer menu that would tempt even the most confirmed beer-o-phobe.

WELCOME TO BEER PARADISE!

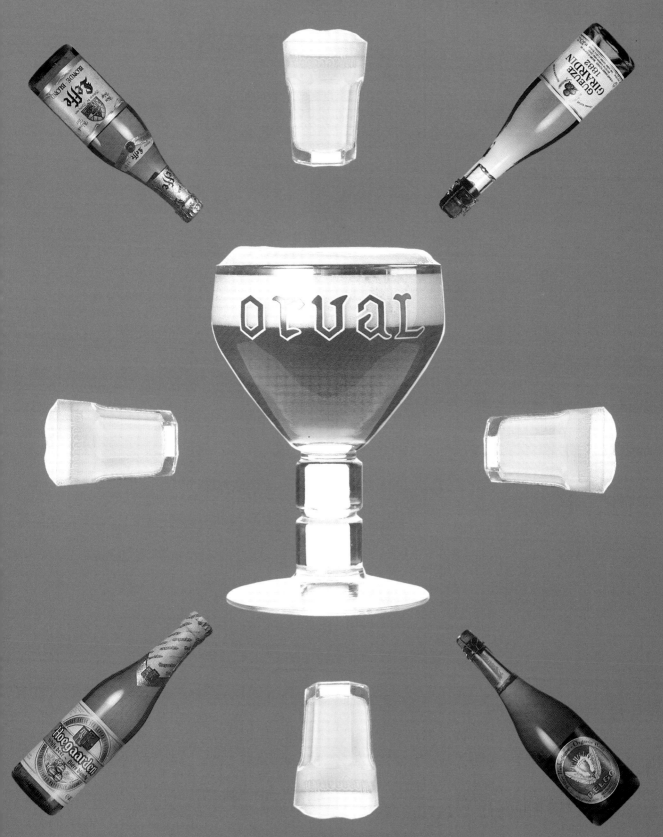

A BRIEF HISTORY OF BELGIAN BEERS

WERE THE PYRAMIDS BUILT WITH BEER?

It is believed that beer was first fermented by Egyptian slaves using bread and water. We would not go so far as to state that "beer built the Pyramids," but we sure would like to!

CHEERS CAESAR!

Beer has been brewed in Belgium ever since the days of the Roman conquest. Gauls and Romans alike enjoyed drinking a Belgian brew that was a somewhat upgraded version of the Egyptian predecessor. It was called *cervoise*.

MONKS: THE FIRST BELGIAN BREWERS

The technical knowledge needed to produce the cereals for brewing beer was concentrated within the walls of the monasteries. The 11th-century monks in the Low Countries, whose orders originated in France, had a great deal of wine-making knowledge and were somewhat astute in the sciences of those times. The monks applied some of their wine-making techniques to brewing and produced the first wholesome Belgian beers. The Affligem Monastery, for example, was brewing as far back as 1083. The Floreffe Monastery started brewing in 1121. Beer was believed to be a healthy alternative to the poor state of the drinking water. It also made fasting a whole lot more fun.

To this day, some monasteries are still brewing beer. There are still six Trappist monasteries that have monks brewing beer. Five of those six are in Belgium.

BEER GUILD

The flourishing interest in brewing quickly manifested itself. A small group of Master Independent Brewers created a Guild to ensure that quality standards were adhered to. In 1450 the first Brewers' Guild of the Low Countries was established. In 1660 almost 100 Brew Masters were officially recognized by the Guild. At that point, Belgium became the most influential brewing area in northern Europe. Apparently, more than 25% of all cereals produced in this region in the 16th century were used for beer making.

DISASTROUS FRENCH RULE

In 1796 Napoleon decreed that all monasteries should be banned and destroyed. This, needless to say, put a total end to monastery brewing. The next 40 years had a devastating effect on beer making in Belgium due to large scale civil unrest and wars. Most of the monasteries were destroyed and never rebuilt. Luckily the Chimay and Rochefort monasteries were rebuilt in the mid-19th century. Today they produce some of the world's highest-quality beers.

THE COMEBACK YEARS: THE BEER REVOLUTION

After the Brabançonne Revolt and Belgium's independence from foreign rule, the brewing industry started its own revolution. The arrival of the industrial age

48

and modern technology played a huge role in both bigger and better production techniques. The 19th century is recognized in Belgium as the brewery boom period or the Beer Revolution. Fortunately, spurred on by laws forbidding consumption of strong spirits, beer drinking and brewing in Belgium has further developed this cultural heritage and an ever-growing demand for beer to be exported worldwide.

THE CHERISHED CHERRY BEER

Without any strict brewing regulations like the German purity laws for beer making *(Reinheitsgebot)*, the Belgians felt free to experiment with the best natural products available. The cherries of Schaarbeek, on the outskirts of Brussels, were used to assist fermentation for a rather unusual sour beer called *gueuze* or *lambic*. At the end of the 19th century this beer was very popular and often drunk on long summer Sunday afternoons (and, indeed, any other afternoon). It was known as beer champagne. Not to leave out the ladies—who were not so keen on the sour base beer—the brewers added the famous local cherries to produce the first fruit beer, *Kriek* (Flemish for cherry), which rapidly became a Brussels' speciality. Later, raspberries and blackcurrants were introduced to produce some rather exciting beer tastes.

THE VAN DE VELDE REGULATION

By 1919, widespread alcoholism within work forces prompted the Belgian minister Emile Van de Velde to prohibit all sales of spirits in public bars in Belgium. This created a huge vacuum for the production of a strong alcoholic drink that was not classed as a spirit. Brewers gladly felt obliged to start producing beers strong in alcohol content. Because this law remained in effect until 1983, Belgian brewers have continued to brew very strong beers. If you look at the Belgo beer list you will find that the average beer is around 6.8% alcohol volume. Bush beer is at a serious 12% alcohol volume. Thank you very much Monsieur Van De Velde for putting our own work force in peril!

DON'T MENTION THE WAR!

The war years saw the invasion of foreign beers into Belgium. During the First World War, the Germans brought their pils with them. Instead of being resentful, the Belgians were only too glad to acquire a new type of beer for their rapidly growing beer portfolio. The first Belgian pils was brewed in 1928 by the Alken Brewery. *Danke schön!* In the Second World War, the British introduced pale ales and Scotch-type beers. This time Belgian brewers experimented and produced a lethally strong golden ale appropriately named Duvel, meaning "the devil!" These new styles of brewing were particularly popular throughout the 50's and 60's.

THE 70'S REVOLT AND REVIVAL

With plenty of civil unrest, strikes, and huge language disputes between the Flemish and Walloons, the Belgian brewers were not about to watch from the sidelines and miss such a great marketing opportunity. The time was ripe for the revival of traditional, regional, and national (flag waving) brewing techniques. Strong, "academic-style" traditional brewing fronts waged battle against mass production of the foreign-style beer. Hey, it was crazy beer names for crazy times: Kwak, Delirium Tremens, Lucifer, Barbar are just a small sample of those far-out beer brands. In 1977, Michael Jackson (the English Beer Hunter), was the first person to publish, in the English language, a tribute to the outstanding quality and diversity of Belgian beer making.

THE 1980'S: A DECADE OF THE BELGIAN BEER

The traditional brewing revival of the 70's never lost its momentum and continued to inspire the reintroduction of traditional beer craftsmanship. In 1986, the Confederation of Belgian Brewers declared the year *"L'Annee de la Bière"* (the year of the beer). Catchy, eh? This created a massive press interest in brewing technology and presentation and the Belgian brewers used the platform as a springboard to launch themselves for global recognition. Exports skyrocketed.

THE 1990'S: BELGIAN BEER *UBER ALLES*!

Today, Belgian beers are the inspiration for all new budding young brewing masters and aficionados: They are the global bench mark for quality brewing. The recent popularity of "micro-brewers," particularly in America, was mainly inspired by the simple, old and natural ways of brewing beer that have been practiced in Belgium for hundreds of years. Thousands of tourists, from Japan to South Africa, visit the beer museums, monasteries, and breweries of Belgium every year. We hope that Belgo shares a little responsibility in having introduced these wonderful beers to a very appreciative public.

BELGO BEER TYPE AND PAIRIN

TYPE	BRAND	COLOR
1. Pils	Jupiler, Maes	pale
2. White Beer	Hoegaarden	white/cloudy
3. Gueze/Lambic	Girardin, Mort Subite	champagne gold
4. Fruit Beers	Liefmans, Belle-Vue	fruit color
5. Pale Ales	DeKonick	copper
6. Golden Ales	Duvel	golden
7. Flemish Brown Ales	Gouden Carolus	dark brown
8. Wine Beers	Rodenbach	dark red
9. Saison	Saison Dupont	cloudy
10. Trappiste	Orval, Chimay	dark, copper
11. Abbey Style	Leffe	gold or dark
12. Specialty	Kwak	amber/orange

HART

Belgo

COOKING USES	FOOD PAIRING
mussel sauce, batter	shellfish
fish sauce	seafood
stews/sauce	soft cheese
game marinade	game
stew eels	filet americain
fish sauce	freshwater fish
dessert	rabbit/chocolate
game/fowl	brown shrimp
pork/choucroute	stoemp
stews/sauces	wild mushrooms
fish sauce	seafood
sauce for fowl	game/fowl

DENIS and ANDRÉ's
GUIDE TO POURING BEER

1 Open the bottle very gently so as not to disturb any sediment and allow it to breathe.

2 Inspect the glass to be sure it is clean by holding it up to the light.

3 Be sure to remove any smears from around the rim and polish carefully with a clean cloth.

4 Pour the nectar gently into the beautiful clean glass to ensure a good head is formed.

5 Drink the beer slowly, letting it sit on the palate before swallowing.

NOW LEVITATE JUST LIKE A MONK!

LAMBIC AND GUEUZE

LAMBIC is a very old-fashioned style of beer, made by an ancient technique that survives only in Belgium—indeed, only in the area around Brussels. No yeast is added to the beer at any stage, other than the wild yeasts that fall from the air onto the cooling wort (the liquid resulting from boiling the grains, hops, and water). This technique is known as spontaneous fermentation.

While many of the world's beers are made entirely from malted grain (most commonly barley), lambic must contain at least 30% unmalted wheat. The hops used are not fresh hops; indeed, they may be several years old. They are not added for their aroma or bitterness, as in other styles of beer, but solely for their preservative qualities.

Lambic continues to ferment and mature in wooden barrels, and emerges very still, and very sour. It is so unlike most other beers that it is considered not to be to the modern taste, and is quite rare.

Gueuze is made by blending old lambic with young lambic and then bottling it. The sugars remaining in the young lambic spark a refermentation in the bottle, very like the secondary fermentation in a bottle of Champagne. The resulting beer is sometimes called Champagne beer: It is very spritzy and is usually bottled with a Champagne cork and wire.

Gueuze is naturally sour with a hint of bitterness, and this is the way it is still made by the traditional, small, family-owned breweries. Drinkers in Belgium often add a dash of grenadine syrup to take the edge off the sourness. When larger companies started to sell gueuze they sweetened it to make it more widely acceptable.

Whichever way you prefer it, gueuze is always refreshing and, compared to wine and other Belgian beers, low in alcohol. The Champagne-style bottle suggests that it is a good aperitif. It goes very well with lamb, chicken, and apple dishes, and is an amazing partner to anything involving vinaigrette, especially the thick, herb and shallot Belgo version.

Belle-Vue
5.2% A comparatively sweet, widely available gueuze.

Cantillon
5.5% A very tart, traditional gueuze.

De Troch
5.5% Dark in color, this is a good example of a full-flavored, sour gueuze. Unfortunately, it is not always available from the brewery.

Girardin
5% Traditional gueuze, slightly sour and citric, with lemon fruitiness and a dry, bitter finish.

Mort Subite
4% Light-bodied and refreshing, sweet/sour.

56

BELGO'S TOP 10 BEERS

FROM BELGIUM

1. ORVAL
2. DE KONICK
3. ENAME TRIPLE
4. TRIPLE WITKAP
5. SLAG PILS
6. DENTERGEMS
7. MAREDSOUS 6
8. LIEFMANS FRAMBOISE
9. CHIMAY GRANDE RESERVE
10. SIXTUS 8

WHITE BEERS

WHITE BEER, known to Belgians as witbier or bière blanche, is so-called because of its distinctive cloudy white appearance, caused by the yeast sediment mixing with the beer. The type of yeast used adds a refreshing lemony tartness. If it were poured too gently from the bottle it would look like a golden beer, but the yeast sediment is what gives white beer its characteristic color and flavor. At Belgo we recommend Hoegaarden on tap, which we reckon gives the best mix of beer and yeast.

White beer is sometimes known as wheat beer: It is brewed from a mixture of malted barley and unmalted wheat (unlike German wheat beers, which use 100% malted grains), to which herbs and spices may be added, such as cilantro and curaçao orange peels.

It is traditional to the eastern part of Belgium, around Leuven, a rural area where a lot of wheat is grown. The spices may sound surprising, but they're not really. In the 18th century, Belgium's Dutch neighbors, who had a great navy and colonies in the Far East, were well known for spice trading, and herbs and spices were used to flavor beer long before hops.

This style of beer had almost died out until it was revived in the 1960s by Pierre Celis at his brewery in the small town of Hoegaarden. White beer became so popular that it was soon being made by other breweries all over Belgium. The Hoegaarden brewery was eventually taken over by a much larger company and Pierre Celis moved to America, where Belgian-style white beers have been rapidly gaining fans.

Light in color and alcohol, this refreshingly tart, fruity beer is often drunk as an aperitif, sometimes with a slice of lemon to enhance the tartness. It is excellent to accompany fish and shellfish, and is used a lot in cooking because it is aromatic and fruity, without any hoppy bitterness. Try adding a splash to sauerkraut just before serving.

Blanche de Namur
4.5% Spicy and slightly bitter.

Dentergems Witbier
5% Dry and refreshing, less spiced than other white beers.

Florisgaarden wit
5% Spritzy and slightly sour.

Hoegaarden Blanche
5% The classic of the style: Tart, fruity, and refreshing cloudy white beer, brewed with cilantro and curaçao orange peels.

Titje
5% Light and fruity.

Vlaamsch Wit/ Blanche des Flandres (Flemish white)
4.5% Sweetish, fruity, and slightly smoky.

FRUIT BEERS

IN THE AREA around Brussels, there is a long tradition of a Sunday afternoon family walk, ending at a bar. The men would order lambic or gueuze (see page 56), but these on their own were considered too sour for women. Instead, they could be sweetened with sugar or grenadine, or flavored with fruit. The locally grown fruit would have been either the rather sour, dark red variety of cherry known as kriek, or raspberries (framboise in French, frambozen in Flemish).

The traditional method was to macerate the whole fruit in lambic beer, which gave it a deep red color. However, it is now commonplace—and far easier for large-scale brewers—to use a mixture of fruits and juices, or essences, to achieve a sweeter, more aromatic flavor.

Kriek and framboise beers were dying out in the 1960s and 1970s, when they were still considered "women's drinks." Their fortunes were revived when other fruit beers—low in alcohol, sweet, and easy to drink—appeared on the market and a wider public rediscovered the originals. Peach and blackcurrant were the earliest of the new fruit beers, but there is now scarcely a fruit that has not been used to flavor beer.

Not all fruit beers are based on lambic. Flemish brown ales (see page 68) and white beers (see page 58) are also used.

In the bars around Brussels, the traditional snack to go with lambic and gueuze-type beers is *plattekaas*, a slightly acidic soft white cheese. It is served with bread and, usually, radishes, although sometimes a sprinkling of cassonnade (soft brown sugar) replaces the radishes.

Fruit beers make wonderful aperitifs, especially if served in Champagne glasses. They are naturals with, or as an ingredient in, desserts, but in fact they work well as an ingredient in many dishes because the acidity of the lambic-based beers cuts cleanly through heavy sauces. For the same reason they are a good choice after a huge, Belgo-style meal; light, refreshing, and sourish, they take the place of sorbet.

Belle-vue Frambozen
5.4% Sweet raspberry taste and syrupy aroma.

Belle-vue Kriek
5.2% Light-bodied, with cherry fruitiness.

Chapeau Banana, Strawberry, Pineapple, or Plum Lambic
3% Sweet and light fruit-flavored beers.

Florisgaarden Ninkeberry
3% White beer base with mangoes and apricots, very sweet.

Liefmans Frambozen
5.2% Flemish brown ale with raspberries, very aromatic.

Liefmans Kriek
6.5% Flemish brown ale with cherries, sweet and fruity.

Liefmans Gluhkriek
6.5% Belgium's answer to mulled wine. Cherry and spice flavored, best served warm with a cinnamon stick.

St Louis Cassis
4.5% Like a Kir Royale, but based on Belgian beer, not French wine. Sweet blackcurrant aroma and sourish flavor.

St Louis Pêche
3.5% Full of peachy fruit flavor, light, sweet/sour.

TRAPPIST BEERS

ONLY A BREW made at a Trappist monastery can use the word Trappist on its label. It is an appellation of origin, though not of style, since the monasteries are dotted around Belgium, and the beers come in a variety of colors and strengths. However, all the beers are strong in alcohol, top-fermented (in other words, they use an ale yeast), and bottle-conditioned, with plenty of yeast sediment and a fruity, aromatic flavor.

The Trappist order is one of the strictest, with closed communities where women may not enter. There are five Trappist monasteries in Belgium: Orval, Chimay, Rochefort, Westmalle, and Westvleteren. Westvleteren is not as commercial as the others, and its beers, sold as Sixtus, are notoriously difficult to get hold of, unless you happen to live near the monastery. The only other Trappist brewery in the world is Schaapskooi in the Netherlands.

Although the Trappist monasteries have long historical links (Orval was founded in the 12th century and Rochefort in the 13th), the ales were mainly developed in the 19th century, and Orval's beer was first brewed in 1931.

With the exception of Orval, each of the Trappist breweries has a beer that is dark brown, rich, and sweetish: This style is sometimes known as double or dubbel. These are definitely the beers to go with game, red meat, and winter casserole dishes. They are sometimes used to cook mussels and rabbit, in which case they can accompany the dish. The paler beers are mostly too strong to drink as aperitifs, but can be served with seafood. The strongest Trappist beers are good with strong cheeses and perfect as after-dinner drinks.

To appreciate the wonderfully complex aromas and flavors, these beers should be drunk at room temperature: About 54-60°F.

Chimay Rouge

7% Dark, very fruity and yeasty, with something of a sweet/sour character.

Chimay Blonde

8% Pale, dry, hoppy, and fruity.

Chimay Bleue

9% Dark, fruity, and spicy; huge character.

Chimay Grande Reserve

9% Vintage Chimay Bleue served in a Champagne-corked bottle. The beer writer Michael Jackson has suggested this is the ideal accompaniment to Roquefort or Stilton cheese.

Orval

6.2% Amber-colored, very dry with a bitter orange aroma and flavor. Its hop character makes it an excellent aperitif, and it is also good with fish and with Belgo's ragout de champignons, made with Orval beer and Orval cheese.

Rochefort 6

7.5% Dark amber to brown, fruity, with some unusual yeasty flavors.

Rochefort 8

9% Tawny-brown, rich, and fruity.

Rochefort 10

11.3% Dark, powerful, sweet, with notes of bitter chocolate. This could be served as a dessert beer with a dessert of Belgian chocolate.

Sixtus 8

10% The beer made at Westvleteren abbey is, on rare occasions, available outside of Belgium. This is one of our favorite beers: It's one of the most full-bodied beers you will ever taste, with the bitterness and slight sweetness of dark chocolate. It is almost a meal in itself, but is not overwhelming: The perfect drink for a cold winter night.

Westmalle Dubbel

6% Dark, soft, and malty, with a hint of spiciness.

Westmalle Tripel

8% A world classic. Golden, strong, with a huge complexity of flavors. It is good with seafood, and is the perfect accompaniment to the plump, white, best Belgian asparagus.

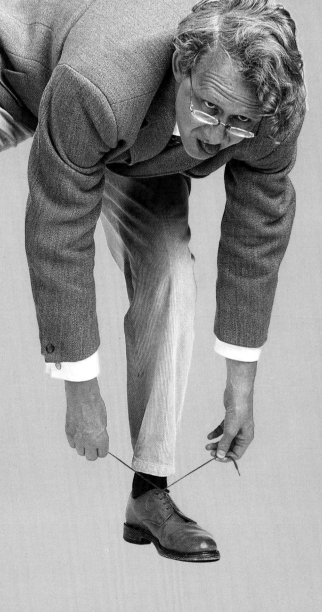

How does a Belgian tie his shoelace?

BROUWERIJ
DE KLUIS
HOEGAARDEN

63

ABBEY BEERS

THERE ARE SEVERAL MONASTERIES in Belgium that are not of the Trappist order, but none of them has made beer for many years. However, several of them license commercial breweries to produce beers for them. Most of these beers are similar in style to the Trappist beers (see previous page). Other breweries make beers that hint at a religious connection, perhaps with labels showing abbeys or monks. None of these beers can use the word Trappist and should be labeled with the word abbey (abbaye in French, *abdij* in Flemish).

Belgium has hundreds of these beers, in very varying styles (and quality); obviously, we at Belgo have selected the best. Like the Trappist ales, abbey beers are strong and top-fermented; some are of an almost unbearable potency and sweetness.

Affligem Triple

8.5% Golden, malty, sweet, and full.

Augustine

8% Deep amber, malty aroma and clean taste.

Bornem Tripel

9% Golden, with a sweet malty aroma, full body, and bitter aftertaste.

Brugse Tripel

9.5% Deep golden with a malty aroma; strong, full-bodied, and sweet.

Corsendonk Agnus

8% Blond, fruity, and slightly bitter.

Corsendonk Pater

8% Dark, with caramel sweetness.

Ename Double

6.5% Dark, sweet, and malty.

Ename Triple

9% Golden, spicy, and bitter.

Floreffe Tripel

8% Golden, strong, and full, with a sweetish aroma and bitter aftertaste. Floreffe is an abbey near Namur; its beers are made by one of Belgium's best small breweries.

Het Kapitel Abt

10% Very full-bodied beer, with a tanginess characteristic of its brewery.

Het Kapitel Pater

6.5% The lightest beer in this range; dark, tangy, with hints of sweetness.

Het Kapitel Prior

9% Golden, sweet, and sour.

Leffe Blonde

6.5% Pale, full-bodied, malty aroma, dry, fruity taste.

Leffe Brune

6.3% Brown, full-flavored, soft, fluffy, creamy, and bitter-sweet.

Maredsous

6% (draft), 6.8% (bottled) Amber-colored and well-balanced, with a delicate floral-fruity perfume and soft, clean malt character. Made for the Benedictine abbey of Maredsous at Anhée-Denée, south of Namur.

Moinette Blonde

8.5% Spicy and full-bodied, with a citrus aroma and very complex, sweet-sour and bitter flavor.

Postel Double

7% Dark, rich, and chocolatey.

St Benoit Brune

6.5% Dark, strong, and sweet.

Steenbrugge Double

6.5% Dark and sweet.

Triple Moine

8% Golden, full, strong, and malty.

Witkap Double

7% Dark, light, and sweetish.

Witkap Stimulo

6% Pale and light-bodied yet full of flavor, with a powerful, fruity aroma.

Witkap Tripel

7.5% Golden, strong, full-bodied, with a fruity aroma and bitter aftertaste.

PALE ALES

LIKE AMERICAN pale ales, these are copper-colored, top-fermented beers, but don't compare the Belgian brews to the American! Belgian beers have a distinctive malt character and yeasty fruitiness, and are usually more carbonated and spritzy, and spicily, rather than hoppily, aromatic. In some bars you can add even more yeast to enhance the flavor. In Belgium, each of the main brands keeps within its territory: De Koninck in and around Antwerp, Straffe Hendrik in Bruges.

They are very easy-drinking beers, on their own, with a bowl of frites and steak tartare (the classic partners in Antwerp), or with fried fish.

Artevelde
5.7% Light and sweetish, with a bitter finish.

De Koninck
5% (draft or bottled) A classic, rounded, malty ale.

De Koninck Cuvée
7.7% Originally a commemorative beer brewed for Antwerp '93 (Antwerp's year as European city of culture). Slightly sweeter than the regular version.

Speciale Op-ale
5% Malty, fruity, and slightly sweet beer with a big head of white foam. Made by De Smedt in the town of Opwijk, northwest of Brussels.

Straffe Hendrik
6% Pale golden color, wheaty aroma, light-bodied, slightly sweet, and tangy with a bitter finish.

Vieux Temps
5.5% ("Old Times") The most popular ale in Wallonia and widely available in Brussels; fruity and yeasty.

Belgium, rather like Britain, has hundreds of breweries, each with strong local support. Some of them produce beers that form a stylistic group, making it a little easier to choose the sort of beer you want to drink.

SEASONAL BEERS (SAISONS)

TRADITIONAL TO THE PROVINCE of Hainaut in southern Belgium (Wallonia), a very agricultural area, saisons (seasons) were made by farmer-brewers in the late fall and winter when there was less farm work. In the days before refrigeration this was also the best time of year for brewing: In hot weather the fermenting beer would spoil. The beers were intended to be drunk in the fields during the following spring and summer. Saisons, therefore, have to be strong enough to last the season yet light enough to be quenching.

It is a very old style and is not always to modern tastes. The beers were partly fermented in wooden casks and may have begun to oxidize, giving a strange, almost "off" flavor which is characteristic of the style. Other weird, yet wonderful, flavors came from small proportions of spelt (a type of wheat), large amounts of hops to preserve the beer, and often a handful of spices for good measure.

Saisons remain a very refreshing style of beer and are very good with basic rustic food, from charcuterie to sauerkraut to stews of beef, pork, or lamb with potatoes or cabbage.

Belgo Blonde
5.5% Organic beer brewed in Belgium by Dupont. Spicy, hoppy aroma, with a light, pleasant bitterness in the finish.

Dupont
6.5% Classic beer from a classic brewery, aromatic and spicy.

Pipaix
6.5% Very aromatic, spicy, tart, and dry.

Saison Silly
5% Light and refreshing, traditional Wallonian beer.

WINE BEERS (RED BEERS)

FLEMISH BROWN ALES (OUD BRUIN)

VELVETY SMOOTH, with a burnt aroma, red beers, a regional speciality of West Flanders, are known as the Burgundies of Belgium. The clear, wine-like color is derived from a particular type of barley and malt, as well as from the tannins and caramels extracted from the Polish oak casks in which the beers mature.

The beers have an oaky quality, and a peculiar, even vinegary sourness deriving from bacteria that live in the wood casks. Some people don't like this sourness, but others love it, and find it a most refreshing, summery beer. Some drinkers add grenadine syrup to soften the tartness.

Rodenbach, made in Roeselare, is the classic example, and in its home province of West Flanders there is a delightful custom of buying a bag of brown shrimp from the fishmonger, then going to a bar and ordering a Rodenbach to drink with the shrimp.

These are excellent aperitif beers and are very useful in cooking. They are also good as an accompaniment to sweetish stews, such as Rabbit in Kriek (see page 82), or dishes cooked in Trappist ale; the red beer gives a delicious sweet-sour effect.

Bacchus
4.5% Fruity and lactic aroma; sweet and sour taste.

Rodenbach Grand Cru
6.5% Fruity and oaky, with a sweet aroma and refreshingly sour taste.

TRADITIONAL TO EAST FLANDERS,"Old brown" ales are generally reddish brown and have a distinctive sourish flavor. These characteristics are a result of several factors: Dark malts and roasted grains are boiled for a long time, giving a hint of caramelization; the region's water is high in sodium bicarbonate; and beer-friendly bacteria live in the wooden maturation casks.

The classic of the style was Liefmans Goudenband, originally made in the town of Oudenaarde. With commercialization it lost a lot of its sourness and it has become a sweeter beer. While the original sourish style was the perfect partner to rustic meat dishes and stews, the more commercial sweeter style is often great with chocolate.

Bios Vlaamse Bourgogne
6% ("Flemish Burgundy") Light, sourish, and slightly fruity.

Liefmans Goudenband
8% Although now leaning to the sweet rather than the sour, this is still a world-class ale.

Liefmans Oud Bruin
5% Sweet and very smooth.

Gouden Carolus
7.5% An excellent after-dinner drink, rich, sweet, and full. Malty aroma, lightly hoppy, with a creamy texture.

Roman Special
5.5% Mellow and slightly bitter.

GOLDEN ALES

ALTHOUGH SIMILAR to beer in color, Belgian golden ales are strong, aromatic, and full of fruit and hops. Their alcoholic complexity is often developed through an elaborate triple fermentation process.

The original of the style is Duvel, made by Moortgat. It was once a dark strong ale, in imitation of the Scotch ales that became popular in Belgium after World War I, but in 1968 the brewery created a golden version that was as tempting as the devil (*duvel* in a Flemish dialect). Its many imitators acknowledge the original in their choice of name.

These golden ales should be served quite cold. Because of their strength they are best enjoyed as a drink on their own. If you feel you need food to avoid a knock-out effect, try them with mussels or an eel dish.

Delirium Tremens
9% Malty aroma, full and sweet with a bitter finish.

Duvel
8.5% Strong and malty, with a bitter hop aftertaste.

Lucifer
8% Full-bodied with a citrus and wheat aroma and bitter finish.

Piraat
10.5% ("Pirate") Malty and very strong.

Sloeber
7.5% ("Joker") Full and strong, extra smooth with a malty aroma.

SPECIALITY BEERS

These are some of Belgium's regional specialities that are difficult to place within any category; their colors, strengths, styles, and tastes are unique.

Affligem Noel

7% Dark, rich, and chocolatey.

Arabier

8% Pale amber with a hoppy aroma and a bitter aftertaste.

Barbar

8% Strong amber ale brewed with honey, giving a slightly sweet flavor.

Brigand

9% Strong, dark, amber-colored, full-bodied and malty.

Bush

12% Belgium's strongest ale, similar to Britain's barley wine but— we think—easier to drink.

Campus Amber

7% Amber-colored, sweetish ale.

Campus Gold

6% Blonde, malty, and sweetish.

Chateau des Flandres

8% Dark, bitter-sweet, and spicy.

Dikkenek

5% Dark ale brewed with juniper berries.

Dupont Xmas

9.5% Well-made, full-bodied, dark, spicy ale.

Flierefluiter

7% Blond, full-bodied, and sweetish; slightly bitter finish.

Gordon Christmas

8.8% Dark, strong, and warming. Brewed in Belgium but based on Scottish "heavy" ale.

Green Dragon

5.5% Bright green! A blend of 17 herbs is used in making this beer.

Hoegaarden Grand Cru

8.7% Pale golden with a honey aroma and taste. It is not a wheat beer, but is seasoned with cilantro and curaçao orange peels.

Julius

8.8% Golden ale with a green apple aroma.

Kasteel

11% ("Castle") Strong, slightly fruity, very warming to sip.

La Divine

9.5% Amber, strong, full, bitter-sweet, and spicy.

La Gauloise Brune

9% Dark, strong, and chocolatey.

McGregor

6.5% Dark, sweet, and smoky. Uses peat-smoked malts, like those used in whiskey-making.

Oerbier

7% Dark, smooth, creamy, and sweet with hints of ripe strawberries.

Pauwel Kwak

8% Dark, full, and warming with a light licorice taste. Served in its specially designed miniature "yard of ale" glass.

Poperings Hommelbier

7.5% (Hop-beer) Amber-colored, strong, creamy, spicy, and very hoppy.

Scotch Silly

8% Strong Scotch-style ale: Reddish-brown, sweet and nutty, full-bodied, warming, and superbly rounded.

Verboden Vrucht

9% ("Forbidden fruit") Strong, dark, rich, and complex, with sweet, spicy, and fruity flavors; surprisingly easy drinking.

PILSNERS

THE WORLD'S FIRST clear golden beer was brewed in 1842 in Pilsen, Bohemia (now part of the Czech Republic). At about the same time, mass-produced glassware was replacing stone drinking vessels. The world could see how good this beer was, and almost immediately began to copy the technique. Every country has its golden beers, and Belgium is no exception, although Belgium, with its enormous choice of individual ales, held out against the Pilsner invasion until the 1920s.

When Belgian brewers started to make Pilsners, they made them well. They are golden colored with a high hop content, which gives the beer a good bite, delicate hop aroma, and elegant hoppy dryness of flavor.

Bel Pils
5.3% Bavarian-style Pilsner with a great hop character.

Jupiler
5.2% Belgium's No 1-selling beer.

Riva Pils
5% Light with a sweet aroma and slightly bitter aftertaste.

Slag Lager
4.8% Light, hoppy, and fruity; matured in the traditional way for 60 days. The name derives from the brewery that makes it, Slaghmuylder.

BIÈRE, BIER, BIRRA, CERVEZA, BEER!

ORVAL

"SLAG,,

CHIMAY

Vieux-Temps

La Cuisine
à la Bière

BEER IS TO THE BELGIANS what wine is to the French and Italians. In fact, it is a whole lot more than that. The English associate Belgium mainly with chocolates and the highway route to their true Euro destination (i.e., France, although hopefully Belgo has helped to change this image). But to the rest of Europe, Belgium means *moules*, *frites,* and *bière*.

One of the most important aspects that distinguishes French *cuisine du terroir* from the Belgian repertoire is that Belgians cook and marinate a great deal with their fabulous beers. *Lapin à la kriek (*rabbit cooked in cherry beer), *pintadeau à la framboise* (guinea fowl in raspberry beer), *huîtres à la gueuze* (oysters in sweet sour beer), *carbonade flamande* (beef stewed in fruit and beer): These are just a few of the more popular dishes in Belgian beer cookery.

ALLEZ—LET'S GO!

Denis and André's
GUIDE TO COOKING WITH BEER

1 In making the marinade, make sure you pour enough beer to cover the meat.

2 Leave meat to marinate 24–28 hours (enough time for a long poker game).

3 Use your beer marinade to cook the meat...very slowly.

4 You should reduce your beer marinade by one-third near the end of cooking.

5 (Above) Add a final glass of beer a few minutes before serving.

6 (Below) Serve meat on plate, pouring beer sauce to cover. Serve with appropriate beer, if there's any left.

LA CUISINE À LA BIÈRE

Soupe à la bière
(Beer soup)

BREWING IN BELGIUM dates back to when the Gauls were bashing up those poor Roman soldiers. In those days they used to drink an alcoholic cereal concoction called *cervoise*. Although brewing never really reached its full popularity in the Lowlands until the 16th century, its reputation was of the highest, and certainly the locals were using beer to cook with before that time.

When brewing finally made its mark, beer replaced wine drinking on a large scale. The Franks, the French Burgundian Court, and the Spanish all brought their wines and wine-making methods into Belgium and made it the official drink of the Courts. But civil wars and religious battles combined with a series of long winters put local brewers under pressure.

Dishes like *carbonade flamandes* date back to medieval times. The beef was originally cooked with water, onions, and thyme. Onions from Flanders were sought after by all of Europe because of their size and sweetness. Although wine was probably used in cooking until it became unobtainable, beer, with its very organic taste, lent itself very well to the stewing of beef. It also proved a better tenderizer than wine. Most of the ancient Belgian dishes were the result of little accidents or folkloric experiments: People using whatever they had, and what was considered good, to cook with. Recipes were passed on as family traditions and rarely written down.

The addition of fruit, such as apples and plums, in cookery came later to enhance taste. It took away some of the bitterness that would come from using the strong local beer. *Cassonade* (brown sugar) or a sweet *pain d'épices* (gingerbread loaf) was sometimes used instead of fruit to both thicken and sweeten at the same time. Some used a slice of brown bread spread with mustard to enhance a dish.

The true *cuisine à la bière* really took off in the mid-19th century with the boom of Belgian brewers and the creation of speciality beers such as *kriek* (cherry beer) and *gueuze* (a sparkling sour beer). Dishes like the *lapin à la kriek* (rabbit in cherry beer) became famous and took their place in the Belgian *repertoire de cuisine* instantly.

Cuisine à la bière is a tradition of using beer as a marinade, sauce base, or as a flavoring. The variety of Belgian beers, which are so distinctive in taste and character, lend themselves perfectly to this concept of cooking. Today this method is more popular than ever and has been further enhanced by the inspiration of Belgium's eccentric brewers. It is only a matter of time before *cuisine à la bière* finds its well-deserved permanent place on the menus of the world's best tables.

SERVES 4

¼ cup butter
2 lbs potatoes, roughly chopped
1 leek, roughly chopped
1 onion, chopped
2 cups Hoegaarden white beer
1 bayleaf and 1 sprig of thyme, tied together
salt and pepper

Melt the butter in a large saucepan, add the chopped potatoes, leek, and onion and cook over low heat for 5 minutes.

Add the beer and 3½ cups water, the herbs and salt and pepper, and simmer for 1 hour.

Remove the herbs, then pass the soup through a vegetable mill or purée in a blender. Reheat and serve hot.

Huîtres à la gueuze
(Oysters in sour beer)

SERVES 2
2 small carrots
2 thin leeks
¼ lb peeled celeriac
salt
12 oysters
3 egg yolks
7 fl oz gueuze beer

Cut the carrots, leeks, and celeriac into very fine strips. Blanch each vegetable separately in salted boiling water for 2-3 minutes. Drain and refresh under cold running water to set the color.

Preheat the broiler.

Protect your hands with thick dishcloths as you open the oysters. Grip each oyster firmly in your palm and keep it level so you do not lose the juice. Insert the tip of your oyster knife into the crack near the hinge of the oyster. Force the knife in and twist to sever the nerve and open the shell. Cut the oyster away from the top and bottom of the shell, then tip the oyster and its juice into a small saucepan. When you have opened all the oysters, poach them in their juice for 1 minute. Remove from the heat and set aside.

Put the egg yolks in a saucepan over very low heat and gradually whisk in the beer. Keep whisking until the sauce thickens, then remove from the heat.

Divide the vegetable strips between two small gratin dishes. Using a slotted spoon, lift the oysters out of their juice and put on top of the vegetables. Pour the beer sauce over the dishes and place under the hot broiler for 30 seconds, until the sauce begins to turn golden brown. Serve at once.

Lotte à la kriek et
aux petits légumes
(Monkfish with cherry beer
and baby vegetables)

SERVES 4
12 baby fennel bulbs
12 baby carrots
12 baby turnips
12 pencil-thin leeks
3½ fl oz fish stock
1 cup kriek / cherry beer
2 bay leaves
2–3 sprigs of thyme
salt and pepper
1½ lb monkfish fillets,
    cut into 1-inch thick slices
3 fl oz cherry paste
3½ fl oz heavy cream

Cook the fennel, carrots, turnips, and leeks in salted boiling water until just tender, then drain and refresh under cold running water. Set aside.

Put the fish stock and beer in a saucepan, bring to a boil and simmer for 10 minutes to reduce the liquid.

Fill a wide saucepan with water, add the bay leaves, thyme, and a pinch of salt. Bring to a boil, then add the monkfish and simmer gently for 5 minutes. Remove the pan from the heat and lift the fish out of the beer using a slotted spoon.

Add the cherry paste and cream to the beer sauce; season to taste and heat through gently.

Reheat the vegetables in a saucepan of boiling water.

Pour the sauce onto four warmed serving plates. Arrange the sliced monkfish in a circle in the center of the plates, with the vegetables around the fish; serve at once.

Coucou de Malines à la Moinette (Chicken with beer, cream, and mustard sauce)

SERVES 2

1 poussin (young chicken), about 2¼ lb
salt and pepper
7 fl oz Moinette beer
1 cup heavy cream
2 teaspoons Dijon mustard

MASHED CELERIAC

½ a celeriac root
2 tablespoons butter

Preheat the oven to 375° F.

Season the chicken inside and out, and roast for about 45 minutes.

Peel and cube the celeriac, boil until tender, then drain and set aside.

Mix half the beer and half the cream with the mustard.

When the chicken is cooked, remove from the oven and let rest for 5 minutes, then cut in half, and keep warm on a plate.

Mash the celeriac and reheat gently with the butter.

Pour the remaining beer into the roasting pan, put over medium heat. Stir to deglaze and loosen the roasting residue. Bring to a boil, add the remaining cream, and simmer for 2–3 minutes, whisking in the mustard mixture.

Serve the chicken on warmed plates with the mashed celeriac and the sauce poured over.

Canard à la bière cassis (Duck with blackcurrant beer sauce)

SERVES 2

1 duck, quartered
2 lbs goose fat
7 fl oz duck stock
3 fl oz cassis / blackcurrant beer
½ cup blackcurrants

Put the duck legs and goose fat on a shallow dish and marinate for 24 hours.

Put the duck legs and goose fat into a saucepan and cook over low heat for 1½ hours or until the meat is very tender.

Boil the duck stock over high heat until reduced by half.

Meanwhile, heat a heavy-bottomed skillet and fry the duck breasts over high heat for about 10 minutes, turning occasionally, until just cooked.

When the stock has reduced to about ½ cup, add the beer and the blackcurrants.

Slice and fan the duck breasts and arrange on two serving plates with the duck legs. Pour the sauce around the duck. Serve with mashed celeriac (see left) and deep-fried shredded celeriac.

Pintade à la framboise
(Guinea fowl in raspberry beer)

SERVES 2

¼ cup butter

1 guinea fowl

salt and pepper

½ large onion, roughly chopped

1 carrot, roughly chopped

1 bay leaf

1 sprig of thyme

1 cup framboise / raspberry beer

3½ fl oz chicken stock

Preheat the oven to 375° F.

Melt the butter in a roasting pan over medium heat. Season the guinea fowl inside and out with salt and pepper, and brown on all sides in the roasting pan. Add the onion, carrot, bay leaf, and thyme and roast in the oven for about 30 minutes.

Remove the guinea fowl from the pan and keep warm.

Pour the beer and stock into the roasting pan. Over medium heat, stir to deglaze and loosen the roasting residue. Bring to a boil and simmer for 10 minutes to reduce the liquid.

Strain the liquid through a conical strainer into a pitcher. Cut the guinea fowl in half and serve on warmed plates, with the sauce poured over. Serve with sautéed potatoes or sauerkraut.

VARIATION
Faisan à la Rodenbach
(Pheasant in Rodenbach red ale)

Use pheasant instead of guinea fowl and replace the raspberry beer with Rodenbach red ale.

Lapin à la kriek
(Rabbit in cherry beer)

SERVES 4

2 rabbits

2 carrots, sliced

2 onions, sliced

2 bay leaves

10 peppercorns

1 cup kriek / cherry beer

2 tablespoons flour

salt and pepper

2 tablespoons peanut oil

1 tablespoon butter

1¾ cups pitted black cherries in natural juices

Cut the rabbits into pieces and use the trimmings to make stock, with 1 carrot, 1 onion, 1 bay leaf, 5 peppercorns, and 2 cups water. Cover and simmer for about 1½ hours, then strain into a pitcher and reserve.

Marinate the rabbit pieces in the beer with the remaining carrot, onion, bay leaf, and peppercorns, for 24 hours. Using a slotted spoon, remove the rabbit from the marinade and pat dry. Coat the rabbit in seasoned flour. Heat the oil and butter in a sauté pan and fry the rabbit until lightly browned on all sides.

Reserve 32 of the black cherries and purée the remainder with a little of the juice.

Remove the saddle pieces and front legs from the pan and add 14 fl oz of the stock, together with the beer marinade and the puréed cherries. Simmer the back legs for about 20 minutes, then return the saddles and front legs to the pan. Salt and pepper to taste, and simmer for a further 20–30 minutes, until the rabbit is tender.

To serve, stir in the reserved cherries with a little of their juice and serve at once, in a soup plate, with boiled potatoes.

Noisettes de chevreuil et poire pochée, sauce à la kriek Liefmans (Noisettes of venison with poached pear and cherry beer sauce)

SERVES 4
2 pears
generous pinch of ground cinnamon
½ cup brown sugar
2 cups Liefmans Kriek / cherry beer
1¼ lb venison steak
salt and pepper
3 tablespoons butter
1 cup cherries in syrup
7 fl oz venison (or veal) stock

Preheat the oven to 400° F.

Peel the pears, cut in half lengthwise, and put in a small saucepan with the cinnamon, sugar, and beer. Simmer until the pears are tender, then remove the pan from the heat, leaving the pears in the liquid.

Season the venison with salt and pepper. Heat the butter in a large oven-proof skillet and lightly brown the venison on both sides, then roast in the oven for 3–4 minutes, until the meat is tender but still pink in the center.

Meanwhile, add half the pear cooking liquid, the cherries, and the venison stock to the pan in which the venison was fried, and simmer for 5–8 minutes.

To serve, slice the pears lengthwise without cutting right through so that they can be fanned out at the top of each plate. Put the venison at the bottom of the plates and pour the sauce over it. Serve at once.

Agneau à la Duvel et gratin dauphinois (Lamb with Duvel beer and gratin dauphinois)

SERVES 4
1¼ lb lamb steaks
salt and pepper
2 tablespoons butter
1½ cups Duvel strong golden ale
7 fl oz lamb stock

GRATIN DAUPHINOIS
4 large potatoes
2 garlic cloves, crushed
1 teaspoon chopped fresh thyme leaves
1 cup milk
7 fl oz heavy cream
freshly grated nutmeg

Preheat the oven to 375° F.

First make the gratin dauphinois. Slice the potatoes very thinly and place in an ovenproof dish. Add the garlic, thyme, milk, cream, nutmeg, and salt and pepper. Cover the dish, and bake in the oven for 45 minutes.

Season the lamb. Heat the butter in a large oven-proof skillet and brown the lamb on both sides, then finish cooking in the oven for 3–4 minutes.

Meanwhile, add the beer and stock to the skillet and simmer gently for 10 minutes.

Divide the potato gratin and lamb steaks between four serving plates and pour over the sauce. Serve at once.

Foie de veau à la Rodenbach (Calves' liver with Rodenbach red ale)

SERVES 4

6 tablespoons butter

2 red onions, thinly sliced

7 fl oz red wine

1½ lb calves' liver, trimmed and thinly sliced

2 tablespoons flour

salt and pepper

1 cup Rodenbach beer

1 cup veal stock

Melt half the butter in a saucepan and sauté the onions for about 5 minutes, until softened but not browned. Add the red wine and simmer for 30–40 minutes, until very soft.

Coat the liver in seasoned flour. Heat the remaining butter in a large skillet over medium-high heat and fry the liver for about 2 minutes on each side, until sealed but still pink in the center. Remove from the pan and keep warm.

Pour the beer and stock into the pan and increase the heat to high. Stir to deglaze the pan and boil until the liquid has reduced and thickened.

Serve the liver on a bed of the red onion mixture, accompanied by stoemp (see page 108) and lentils, and pour the beer sauce over the liver.

Filet de porc à la Westmalle Dubbel (Pork fillet with Westmalle Dubbel Trappist ale)

SERVES 4

6 tablespoons butter

4 potatoes (preferably Cara), cubed

¼ lb Ardennes ham or prosciutto

1½ lb pork fillet

1½ cups Westmalle Dubbel dark Trappist ale

7 fl oz heavy cream

salt and pepper

Preheat the oven to 375° F.

Melt the butter in a sauté pan and sauté the potatoes until lightly browned all over.

Cut the ham or prosciutto into thin strips and sauté with the potatoes for 1–2 minutes, then transfer to an ovenproof dish and bake in the oven for 20 minutes.

Meanwhile, trim the pork and cut into medallions. Season with salt and pepper, and fry until well browned, then bake in the oven for about 8 minutes, or until cooked. Remove from the oven and keep warm.

Pour the beer into the pan in which the pork was fried and simmer for 2 minutes, then add the cream and simmer for another 1–2 minutes. Season to taste.

To serve, put the pork medallions on four serving plates and mound the potatoes on top. Pour the sauce over the meat and serve at once.

Rognons de veau à la Trappiste Chimay Rouge
(Calves' kidneys in Chimay Trappist beer sauce)

SERVES 4

1¾ lb calves' kidneys in their suet
4 tablespoons all-purpose flour
salt and pepper
¼ cup butter
1½ cups Chimay Rouge beer
½ cup veal stock

Cut the kidneys into ½-inch thick slices, leaving a thin layer of suet around the edge. Toss the kidneys in seasoned flour to coat them evenly. Melt the butter in a skillet until it begins to foam, then add the kidneys and fry for 3 minutes on each side.

Remove the kidneys from the skillet and keep warm. Pour the veal stock and three-quarters of the Chimay beer into the pan, bring to a boil and let it reduce to about 7 fl oz. Season to taste. Return the kidneys and any juices to the skillet and heat for 1 minute. Add the remaining Chimay beer and cook for 30 seconds. Serve the kidneys on warmed plates and pour the beer sauce over the kidneys.

Carbonade flamande
(Flemish beef stew)

SERVES 6

3 lb chuck steak, cut into 2-inch chunks
2½ cups Liefmans Goudenband
2 tablespoons peanut oil
2 tablespoons butter
2 tablespoons brown sugar
1 tablespoon freshly grated nutmeg
salt and pepper
3 tablespoons flour
2 tablespoons tomato paste
¾ cup pitted prunes, sliced
14 fl oz veal stock
1 bouquet garni
1–2 tablespoons Dijon mustard
2 cooking apples

Marinate the meat in 1½ cups of the beer for 3 days.

Lift the meat out of the marinade, reserving the marinade. Heat the oil and butter in a large, heavy-bottomed skillet, add the meat, sugar, and nutmeg, and cook over medium-high heat, stirring frequently, until the meat is well browned. Using a slotted spoon, transfer the meat to a casserole dish and season with salt and pepper.

Stir the flour into the oil and butter and cook until well browned, then stir in the tomato paste, prunes, veal stock, bouquet garni, and the beer marinade. Bring to a boil, skim, and then pour over the meat. Simmer very gently until the meat is tender, about 1 hour.

Stir in the mustard and the remaining beer, then taste and adjust the seasoning. Peel and quarter the apples, add to the casserole dish, and cook for 5–10 minutes, until the apples are tender. Serve hot.

Fruits marinés à la bière framboise
Fruit salad with raspberry beer

SERVES 4

1 apple

1 pear

14 fl oz framboise / raspberry beer

⅔ cup sugar

8 mint leaves, finely chopped

12 strawberries

2 bananas

1¼ cups raspberries

It is best to begin making this dish a day in advance. Peel the apple and pear and slice them thinly. Put them in a bowl with the beer, sugar, and chopped mint leaves. Cover and refrigerate overnight.

The following morning, slice the bananas into the bowl and add the raspberries and strawberries. Return to the refrigerator until ready to serve.

Serve the fruit and juices in glass bowls or soup plates, with fresh cream if desired.

Sorbets à la bière
(Fruit beer sorbets)

SERVES 4

1 cup sugar

3 fl oz fruit beer (framboise / raspberry, kriek / cherry, or pêche / peach)

3½ fl oz fruit purée or juice (raspberry, cherry, or peach)

TO SERVE

½ cup fruit purée

sprigs of mint

Put the sugar in a saucepan with 1 cup water and bring to a boil. Boil for 2 minutes, then let cool.

Mix the cold syrup with the beer and fruit purée and put it in an ice-cream maker to process. When the sorbet is firm, transfer it to a freezer container and freeze until required.

To serve, scoop two or three balls of sorbet into each serving bowl and serve with a few tablespoons of fruit purée and a sprig of mint.

Traditional
Belgian dishes

WHEN IT COMES TO their own home cooking, the Belgians have tended to remain purists and have kept their cuisine too much to themselves. This probably stems from years of foreign rule on their home turf. With the rise of Flemish and Walloon nationalism in the seventies, Belgian traditional cooking got the opportunity to raise its regional flags alongside the resurgence of traditional beers. Grandmothers' dishes started to appear not only in popular student cafés but also in all the fashionable restaurants across Belgium.

ALLEZ...ENJOY!

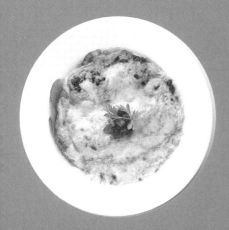

ONE OF BELGIUM's most fashionable restaurants is the Brabançon in the Rue de la Commune in Brussels. This establishment managed to survive the hedonistic eighties, when everything new came in and everything old went out. It remained true to a cuisine that was almost forgotten by the new influx of restaurant-goers. Unfortunately, the decor has not kept up with time, but in our eyes that makes it even more fun. Marie-Jeanne Lucas, proprietor and head chef at the Brabançon, is not too bothered about changing the style of the place: She was awarded the Grand Prix de la Cuisine Artisanale et Régionale. She has also just celebrated her 77th birthday!

Belgo owes much to Marie-Jeanne's time and kindness in sharing her secrets and passion for Belgian traditional cooking. Never mind the rather peculiar paintings of horses laboring the fields that dominate the walls of her restaurant. Never mind the three pug dogs and Titje the parrot. The main reason you are at the Brabançon is to taste true Belgian cuisine in its purist form. When Madame Lucas serves you your pound of butter with a knife stuck through it you know you're in the right place.

Nowadays, many restaurants in Belgium have started to acknowledge that their national cuisine deserves wider recognition and a better place than on the menus of tourist traps. Yes, now even the fashion-conscious Belgians themselves would like to sample some of grandmother's deliciously prepared dishes in less intimate environments than their own homes. The Spinnenkopke, which specializes in *cuisine à la bière*, Le Canterbury, and Le Petit Pont restaurants in Brussels are all fine examples of this new wave of *la cuisine traditionnelle Belge*.

At times, Belgo has been heralded as the true Belgian Embassy in London for its role in promoting Belgian cuisine and beers there, and in doing so promoting Belgian culture, itself. Of course we are very grateful for all the recognition we have received from some of the most widely read Belgian newspapers and magazines, but even more, we are now glad to be just a few minutes away from a *tomates crevettes* or *witloof au gratin*. We hope the following recipes will save you a few plane tickets but not stop you from visiting Belgo.

TYPICAL BELGIAN INGREDIENTS

The most satisfying thing about producing the food for the menus at Belgo is that we do not need to bring our ingredients from far and exotic places. The true beauty of Belgian food is its sublime simplicity.

The ingredients that are used for the recipes at Belgo are typical of those used in traditional Belgian dishes, such as *waterzooi* and *carbonade*. We remain true to the traditional recipes, though we may vary the amount of fat and butter that was once used. Belgians were so renowned for the amount of butter they ate that the government recently issued a warning asking restaurants not to serve dishes such as *raie au beurre noir* (skate cooked in *beurre noisette*), so heavy with butter, because of concern about the Belgian population's cardiac problems. (This problem was originally recorded by one of François I's doctors, who referred to the Belgians as a bunch of *bouffeur de beurre* or butter eaters.

We felt confident that Belgo would succeed because we knew that our guests would feel extremely familiar with ingredients such as leeks, asparagus, potatoes, beets, carrots, fennel, onion, celery, thyme, chives, rosemary, turnips, radish, beef, chicken, fish, butter, and cream, to name but a few. They sound so familiar you would think your grandmother had just opened up a restaurant. It is not so much where and how far you get your ingredients from that is important. Rather it is their freshness and what one does with them that is the substance of making good food.

It's important to note that, since the 14th century, Belgium, together with Holland, has been the "vegetable basket" of Europe. Together the two countries were the first to mass produce and export fresh vegetables. Today they export the largest volume of vegetables in Europe.

Britain owes much to Belgium for the introduction of new vegetables. It was, after all, Belgians from Flanders who introduced the carrot and the turnip to Britain. And the potato was first exported to Britain back in the mid-18th century. Belgium was also responsible for developing many new types of vegetables such as the Brussels sprout, the witloof (chicory or Belgian endive), and hop shoots.

Nowadays, the witloof is omnipresent in Belgian cooking. At Belgo we use it for salads, soups, garnish, mashed, and as a cooked vegetable. The Belgians regard the witloof as their most treasured vegetable. Even the *choux de Bruxelle* cannot match it on presence and recognition. Witloof, braised in butter with a dash of lemon, brown sugar, and nutmeg is bliss! *Witloof au gratin* (braised endive wrapped with ham in bechamel sauce and then gratinéed) is a Belgo top seller.

The leek also holds a particularly high place in the Belgian repertoire. Similar to the endive and a great alternative to the more expensive asparagus, it is used at Belgo in all our vegetable *julienne* and to flavor our fish, as in the *waterzooi de poisson*.

Nutmeg is probably the most important spice in Belgian cuisine. It is used as seasoning rather like pepper, sprinkled on butter-fried vegetables and also to flavor *stoemp* (Belgian mashed potato with cooked vegetables). *Stoemp* is super. You

will find it on any simple traditional Belgian restaurant's menu. It accompanies sausages and meats very well.

Asparagus has been part of the Belgian family meal since the 16th century. Every year in May the white asparagus season starts and in Belgium, Germany, and Holland this is celebrated with great relish. You can stroll into any local restaurant and find that special menus have been set out featuring the white asparagus as an appetizer or for main-course portions. Some restaurants specializing in mussels will use the occasion to replace the seasonal shellfish in this period with asparagus. At Belgo we make sure we have both year round by using green asparagus when the white season ends. You can serve asparagus with almost any sauce. The most typical Belgian way of eating asparagus is steamed, and then cooked in butter with hard-boiled egg and chives.

Tomates farcies de crevettes grises
(Tomatoes stuffed with shrimps and mayonnaise)

SERVES 2

4 tomatoes

1 large bunch of mâche (corn salad)

½ lb peeled brown (Gulf pink) shrimp

1 tablespoon chopped fresh chives

3½ fl oz mayonnaise

4 tablespoons vinaigrette dressing

Bring a saucepan of water to a boil. Using a sharp knife, mark a cross on the bottom of each tomato, then put in the boiling water for 10 seconds. Remove from the pan and refresh under cold running water. Peel the tomatoes, then slice off their tops, and scoop out the seeds and pulp.

Wash and drain the mâche.

Mix the shrimp with the chives and pack about half of them into the tomatoes. Put the tomatoes on two serving plates and top with mayonnaise. Toss the mâche in vinaigrette and arrange it around the stuffed tomatoes, with the remaining shrimp. Garnish with half a lemon.

Crème de chicons à la bière blanche
(Cream of Belgian endive soup with wheat beer)

SERVES 4

4 heads of Belgian endive

¼ cup butter

1 small onion, thinly sliced

4 large potatoes, quartered

¼ cup brown sugar

1 bouquet garni

1 cup white beer

3½ cups chicken stock or water

salt and pepper

freshly grated nutmeg

1 cup heavy cream

Cut the Belgian endive in half lengthwise and cut out the cores. Slice the Belgian endive thinly. Melt the butter in a saucepan, add the onion, and cook for 1 minute. Add the Belgian endive, potatoes, sugar, and bouquet garni, and cook over low heat for 15 minutes.

Add the beer, stock or water, salt, pepper, and nutmeg. Simmer gently for about 1 hour.

Remove the bouquet garni and mix the soup in a blender or pass it through a food mill. Return the soup to the saucepan, add the cream, and bring back to a boil. Taste and adjust the seasoning if necessary. Serve hot.

Coquilles oostendaise
(Scallops with seafood and cream sauce)

SERVES 4

¼ of a celery root (celeriac)

2 small carrots

1 leek

¼ cup butter

8-12 scallops, with 4 shells

3 tablespoons white beer

7 fl oz heavy cream

8-12 mussels, freshly cooked

¼ lb peeled brown (Gulf pink) shrimp

salt and pepper

Peel the celery root and carrots and trim the leek. Cut all the vegetables into very fine (julienne) strips. Melt the butter in a saucepan, add the vegetables, and cook over low heat until they are just tender, but still quite crisp to the bite. Remove and put to one side.

Cut the scallops horizontally into three or four slices (depending on their size). Heat a nonstick skillet and add the scallops; cook for 30 seconds on each side. Remove from the pan and set aside.

Heat the beer in a saucepan over low heat for 2 minutes, then add the cream, mussels, shrimp, and seasoning, and cook for a further 2 minutes.

To serve, preheat the broiler. Divide the vegetables between four scallop shells and put the scallops on top. Pour the sauce over and put under the hot broiler for 30 seconds. Serve at once, with lemon wedges.

Toast cannibale
(Steak tartare crostini)

SERVES 1

¼ lb beef fillet

1 tablespoon finely chopped pickle

1 tablespoon finely chopped shallots

1 tablespoon capers, chopped

1 drop of Tabasco sauce

1 tablespoon mayonnaise

salt and pepper

2 slices of French bread

Finely mince the beef and mix with the chopped pickle, shallots, capers, Tabasco, mayonnaise, and salt and pepper to taste.

Lightly toast the French bread and spread the beef mixture over the bread. If you like, serve with salad leaves, pickles, and pickled onions.

Croquettes de fromage (Cheese croquettes)

SERVES 4

1 envelope unflavored gelatin

1 cup milk

¼ cup butter

1 cup all-purpose flour

1 cup Gruyère cheese, grated

1 cup Cheddar cheese, grated

salt and pepper

freshly grated nutmeg

1 cup fine, dried bread crumbs

2 eggs

vegetable oil for deep frying

bunch of curly parsley

Soak the gelatin in cold water until soft. Heat the milk in a saucepan, then add the softened gelatin. In another saucepan, melt the butter and whisk in ½ cup of the flour; cook over low heat, whisking constantly, for 4 minutes. Gradually add the milk mixture, whisking all the time, and cook for 4–5 minutes.

Remove from the heat and beat in the grated cheeses. Season well with salt, pepper, and nutmeg. Pour the mixture into a 1-inch deep baking pan lined with plastic wrap. Let cool for about 1 hour, then refrigerate to set firm.

Put the bread crumbs and the remaining flour on two plates. Beat the eggs in a mixing bowl. Remove the cheese mixture from the refrigerator and use the plastic wrap to lift it out of the baking pan. Cut the cheese mixture into rectangular pieces, about 4 x 1 inches in diameter.

Dip each piece into the plate of flour, then into the beaten eggs, and finally in the bread crumbs to coat evenly. Refrigerate for 30 minutes.

To serve, heat the oil for deep frying. Deep fry the parsley for 1 minute, until it is crisp, then drain on paper towels. Deep-fry the cheese croquettes for 3–4 minutes, until golden brown. Drain on paper towels. Serve hot, garnished with half a lemon.

Croquettes de crevettes grises (Shrimp and brandy bisque croquettes)

SERVES 4

2 lbs unpeeled brown (Gulf pink) shrimp

1 envelope unflavored gelatin

¼ cup butter

1 cup all-purpose flour

1 tablespoon brandy

1 tablespoon tomato paste

salt and pepper

½ lb peeled brown (Gulf pink) shrimp

1 cup fine, dried bread crumbs

2 eggs

vegetable oil for deep frying

bunch of curly parsley

Put the unpeeled shrimp in a saucepan filled with 2 cups water. Bring to a boil, then put the shrimp and water in a blender and blend until smooth; rub through a strainer.

Soak the gelatin in cold water until soft. Melt the butter in a saucepan and whisk in ½ cup of the flour; cook over low heat, whisking constantly, for 4 minutes. Gradually add the shrimp liquid, whisking all the time. Beat in the brandy, tomato paste, and the softened gelatin. Season well. Cook the mixture until it thickens, then stir in the peeled shrimp.

Pour the mixture into a 1-inch deep baking pan lined with plastic wrap. Let cool for about 1 hour, then refrigerate to set firm.

Put the bread crumbs and the remaining flour on two plates. Beat the eggs in a mixing bowl. Remove the shrimp mixture from the refrigerator and use the plastic wrap to lift it out of the baking pan. Cut the shrimp mixture into rectangular pieces, about 4 x 1 inches in diameter.

Dip each piece into the plate of flour, then into the beaten eggs, and finally in the bread crumbs to coat evenly. Refrigerate for 30 minutes.

To serve, heat the oil for deep frying. Deep fry the parsley for 1 minute, until it is crisp, then drain on paper towels. Deep fry the shrimp croquettes for 3–4 minutes, until golden brown; drain on paper towels. Serve hot, garnished with salad leaves and half a lemon.

Croquettes de poulet (Chicken croquettes)

SERVES 4
2 chicken legs
1 carrot, cut in half
1 onion, cut in half
1 sprig of thyme
1 bay leaf
3 cloves
1 envelope unflavored gelatin
¼ cup butter
1 cup all-purpose flour
1 teaspoon chopped fresh tarragon
¼ cup heavy cream
salt and pepper
1 cup fine, dried bread crumbs
2 eggs
vegetable oil for deep frying
bunch of curly parsley

Put the chicken in a saucepan with 3½ cups water, the carrot, onion, thyme, bay leaf, and cloves. Bring to a boil and simmer for 1 hour.

Remove the chicken and boil the cooking liquid to reduce it to 1 cup. Strain the stock. Meanwhile, cut the chicken meat into small pieces.

Soak the gelatin in cold water until soft. Melt the butter in a saucepan and whisk in ½ cup of the flour; cook over low heat, whisking constantly, for 4 minutes. Gradually add the chicken stock, whisking all the time, and cook the mixture for 5–6 minutes.

Beat in the softened gelatin, chicken pieces, tarragon, and cream; season well. Pour the mixture into a 1-inch deep baking pan lined with plastic wrap. Let cool for about 1 hour, then refrigerate to set firm.

Coat the chicken mixture in flour, eggs, and bread crumbs as for shrimp croquettes. Chill, deep-fry and serve in the same way.

Salade liegeoise
(Warm salad with bacon, new potatoes, and green beans)

SERVES 4

16 new potatoes

1 lbs green beans

8 strips of smoked bacon

1 onion, finely chopped

4 tomatoes, quartered

7 fl oz vinaigrette dressing

2 tablespoons chopped fresh parsley

¾ lb mixed salad leaves

Cook the potatoes and green beans in salted boiling water until just tender. Drain, and refresh the beans in cold running water. Cut the potatoes in half.

Meanwhile, cut the bacon into thin strips and cook under a hot broiler until crisp.

Reheat the potatoes and beans in boiling water, then mix them with the onion, tomatoes, three-quarters of the vinaigrette, and the parsley. Place the mixture in a dome shape on four serving plates and scatter the crisp bacon over the top. Toss the salad leaves with the remaining vinaigrette and arrange around the serving plates.

Witloof au gratin
(Braised Belgian endive with ham and cheese sauce)

SERVES 2

4 heads of Belgian endive

2 tablespoons brown sugar

juice of 1 lemon

salt and pepper

freshly grated nutmeg

2 cups milk

1 bay leaf

10 peppercorns

1 sprig of thyme

1 slice of onion

¼ cup butter

½ cup all-purpose flour

4 slices of proscuitto

½ cup grated Gruyère cheese

½ cup grated Cheddar cheese

Preheat the oven to 450° F.

Cut the cores out of the Belgian endive from the bottom, leaving them whole. Put them in a small baking pan and sprinkle them with brown sugar, lemon juice, salt, pepper, and nutmeg, and add enough water to half cover them. Cover with tin foil and bake for 20 minutes. Remove the tin foil and bake for a further 20 minutes. Turn the Belgian endive and bake for a further 20 minutes. Drain well.

Put the milk in a saucepan with the bay leaf, peppercorns, thyme, and onion, bring to a boil, then set aside.

In another saucepan, melt the butter and whisk in the flour. Cook over low heat, whisking constantly, for 1–2 minutes. Gradually pour in the milk through a strainer, whisking all the time. Bring the sauce back to a boil and cook for 3–4 minutes, whisking constantly until it thickens. Season to taste with salt, pepper, and nutmeg.

Wrap a slice of prosciutto around each head of Belgian endive and put in two individual gratin dishes. Pour the sauce over, sprinkle with the cheese, and heat through in the oven for 15–20 minutes, then put under a hot broiler until the cheese is golden brown and bubbling. Serve hot.

Anguilles au vert
(Eels in green sauce)

SERVES 4

12 new potatoes

2½ cups fish stock

7 fl oz wheat beer

1¾ lb eels

2 bunch of watercress

1 tablespoon chopped fresh dill

1 tablespoon chopped fresh chives

7 fl oz heavy cream

salt and pepper

Cook the potatoes in salted boiling water until just tender.

Put the fish stock and beer in a wide saucepan and bring to a simmer.

Cut the eels into 2-inch pieces, then poach them in the stock for 4–5 minutes. Drain and set aside.

Chop the watercress leaves with the dill and chives as finely as possible, or purée in a blender.

Boil the fish stock to reduce by two-thirds, then add the cream and the watercress purée. Whisk together and season well. Add the eels and potatoes and reheat gently for 3–4 minutes. Serve in soup plates.

Cabillaud à la flamande
(Flemish-style cod)

SERVES 4

20 new potatoes

4 hard-boiled eggs

4 cod steaks, about 6 oz each

salt and pepper

¾ cup all-purpose flour

½ cup butter

2 tablespoons chopped fresh parsley

juice of 2 lemons

Preheat the oven to 400° F.

Cook the potatoes in salted boiling water until just tender. Peel the hard-boiled eggs and chop finely.

Season the cod with salt and pepper, and toss in flour to coat. Heat the butter in a skillet, add the cod, and fry until lightly browned on both sides. Put the fish in an ovenproof dish and bake for about 2 minutes or until cooked through.

Put the skillet over moderate heat, add the egg, and heat through for 1 minute, then add the chopped parsley and lemon juice. Arrange the cod on four warmed serving plates and pour the egg mixture over it. Serve with the boiled potatoes.

Raie au beurre noir
(Skate with black butter)

SERVES 2

10 new potatoes

2 skate (ray) wings, about 10 oz each

½ cup all-purpose flour, seasoned

⅓ cup butter

1 tablespoon capers, rinsed

juice of 1 lemon

1 tablespoon chopped fresh parsley

Preheat the oven to 400° F.

Cook the potatoes in salted boiling water until just tender.

Using scissors, trim the skate wings, removing the outside bones. Toss in the seasoned flour.

Heat the butter in a wide, ovenproof skillet until golden brown. Add the skate wings and cook for 2 minutes on each side or until well colored. Put the pan in the oven for 4–5 minutes or until the fish is cooked through.

Arrange the fish on two warmed serving plates. Put the pan over moderate heat, add the capers, and cook, stirring, for 30 seconds. Add the lemon juice and chopped parsley and pour it over the skate. Serve at once, with the boiled potatoes.

Sole à l'oostendaise
(Sole with mussels and shrimp)

SERVES 4

1¾ cups fish stock

7 fl oz heavy cream

beurre manié (1 tablespoon butter mashed with 1 tablespoon flour until smooth)

7 fl oz wheat beer

2 globe artichokes

1 lemon, cut in half

12 new potatoes

4 lemon sole fillets, about 6 oz each

8-12 mussels, freshly cooked

3 oz peeled brown (Gulf pink) shrimp

COURT BOUILLON

½ cup dry white wine

1 carrot and 1 small onion, sliced

1 sprig of thyme, 1 bay leaf, 3 cloves

For the court bouillon, put all the ingredients in a covered saucepan with 2 cups of water, and simmer for 20 minutes.

Put the fish stock in a saucepan and boil to reduce by half. Add the cream and boil for 1 minute, then whisk in the beurre manié to thicken the sauce. Whisk in the beer.

Snap off the artichoke stems, cut off the leaves, and rub the artichoke bottoms with the lemon. Bring a saucepan of water to a boil, add the lemon halves and artichoke bottoms, and cook for 15–20 minutes, until tender. Refresh under cold running water. Scoop out the chokes with a teaspoon. Boil the potatoes until just tender, then drain and set aside with the artichoke bottoms.

Roll up the fish fillets and hold in place with a toothpick. Poach the fish in the court bouillon for 3–4 minutes, until just cooked, then drain.

Reheat the beer-cream sauce, adding the mussels, shrimp, potatoes, and quartered artichoke bottoms. Remove the toothpicks and arrange the fish on four warmed plates. Arrange the remaining ingredients on the plates and pour the sauce over.

Lotte aux poireaux
(Monkfish with leeks)

SERVES 4

1¼ lb leeks

12 new potatoes

2 cups fish stock

7 fl oz wheat beer

1½ lb monkfish fillet

7 fl oz heavy cream

salt and pepper

Clean the leeks thoroughly and slice them finely. Cook leeks in a saucepan of boiling water for 2 minutes, drain, and refresh under cold running water. Cook the potatoes until just tender, then drain, refresh under cold water, and set aside with the leeks.

Put the fish stock in a saucepan with the beer and boil to reduce the liquid by half.

Cut the monkfish into ½-inch slices and poach in the reduced stock for 2 minutes.

Add the cream, potatoes, leeks, and salt and pepper, and simmer gently for 4–5 minutes. Serve in soup plates.

Poussin à l'estragon
(Tarragon spring chicken)

SERVES 2

2 poussins

salt and pepper

freshly grated nutmeg

2 tablespoons vegetable oil

¼ cup butter

2 sprigs of thyme

½ cup chicken stock

1 tablespoon chopped fresh tarragon

3½ fl oz heavy cream

Preheat the oven to 400° F.

Season the poussins inside and out with salt, pepper, and nutmeg. Heat the oil and butter in a large skillet, add the poussins, and brown on all sides.

Transfer to a flameproof casserole dish and add the thyme. Bake in the oven for 20–30 minutes or until cooked.

Remove from the oven, add the chicken stock and tarragon to the casserole dish, and simmer over medium-high heat until the liquid is slightly reduced. Add the cream and bring back to a boil, then serve at once. Oven-roasted potatoes are the ideal accompaniment.

Poussin à la brabançonne (Spring chicken with genever sauce and caramelized Belgian endive)

SERVES 2

4 heads of Belgian endive
⅓ cup brown sugar
salt and pepper
freshly grated nutmeg
½ cup butter
2 poussins
2 tablespoons vegetable oil
1 fl oz clear genever
3½ fl oz chicken stock

Preheat the oven to 400° F.

Cut the cores out of the Belgian endive from the bottom, leaving them whole. Place on a small baking sheet and sprinkle with brown sugar, salt, pepper, nutmeg, half the butter, and about 4 tablespoons water. Bake in the oven for 45 minutes, turning them halfway through the cooking time.

Season the poussins inside and out. Heat the remaining butter with the oil in a roasting pan, add the poussins, and brown on all sides. Bake in the oven for 20–30 minutes or until cooked.

Remove from the oven, add the clear genever and the chicken stock, and boil for 1 minute.

Arrange the caramelized Belgian endive on warmed plates with the poussins on top. Pour the sauce around them and serve with stoemp (see page 108).

Filet american
(Steak tartare)

SERVES 1

6 oz beef fillet

1½ tablespoons finely chopped pickles

1½ tablespoons finely chopped shallots

1½ tablespoons capers, chopped

2 drops of Tabasco sauce

2 tablespoons mayonnaise

salt and pepper

Finely mince the beef and mix with the chopped pickles, shallots, and capers. Stir in the Tabasco, mayonnaise, and salt and pepper to taste.

Mold the mixture to resemble the shape of a fillet steak and place on a serving plate. Garnish with salad leaves and two or three pickles and small pickled onions. Ideally, serve with frites.

WATERZOOI

Waterzooi aux poissons
(Mixed fish in a cream sauce)

Waterzooi is as Belgian as Tintin. This is a dish that dates back a few hundred years. Waterzooi simply means boiled or stewed in water. It was originally made using freshwater fish and rough cuts of vegetables, which were cooked together in water with thyme and bay leaves. Fresh cream would be added just before serving. The freshwater fish version was later replaced by waterzooi à la gantoise, which uses chicken instead of fish, and lemon and black pepper to flavor.

In fact, this cooking concept permits you to use what you want. At Belgo we also cook our own version of the waterzooi: Aux poissons de la Mer du Nord. This recipe is made with a combination of salmon, sea bass and ocean perch, and crayfish.

SERVES 4
1½ cups carrots
1½ cups celeriac
1½ cups trimmed leeks
2 cups fish stock
7 fl oz wheat beer
7 fl oz heavy cream
12 new potatoes
4 pieces of salmon fillet, about ¼ lb each
4 sea bass fillets, about ¼ lb each
4 pieces of ocean perch fillet, about ¼ lb each
2 teaspoons tomato paste
8–12 mussels, well scrubbed
12 crayfish (preferably live)
salt and pepper
chopped fresh parsley

Peel the carrots and celeriac. Cut all the vegetables into very fine (julienne) strips and cook in separate saucepans of salted boiling water for 2–3 minutes. Drain and refresh under cold running water.

Put the fish stock and beer in a saucepan and boil to reduce by half. Add the cream. Reduce the heat to a simmer, add the potatoes, and cook for 10–15 minutes, until nearly tender.

Add the fish and simmer for a further 5 minutes. Add the tomato paste and mussels and boil for 2 minutes. Add the crayfish and vegetables and cook for 2-3 minutes. Season with salt and pepper and serve in soup plates, sprinkled with chopped parsley.

Waterzooi de lotte
(Monkfish in a cream sauce)

SERVES 4

1½ cups carrots
1½ cups celeriac
1½ cups trimmed leeks
12 new potatoes
2½ cups fish stock
½ cup wheat beer
12 crayfish (preferably live)
1½ lb monkfish fillet, cut into chunks
7 fl oz heavy cream
salt and pepper

Peel the carrots and celeriac. Cut all the vegetables into very fine (julienne) strips and cook in separate saucepans of boiling salted water for 2–3 minutes. Drain and refresh under cold running water. Cook the potatoes until just tender and set aside with the vegetables.

Put the fish stock and beer in a saucepan, bring to a boil, and add the live crayfish, if using. After 2–3 minutes, remove the crayfish and set aside.

Boil the stock until it is reduced by half. Reduce the heat, add the monkfish, and poach for 2 minutes. Add the cream and season to taste. Add the crayfish, vegetables, and potatoes, and heat through for 2–3 minutes. Serve in soup plates.

Waterzooi à la gantoise
(Chicken in a vegetable, cream, and lemon sauce)

SERVES 4

1½ cups celeriac
1½ cups carrots
1½ cups trimmed leeks
12 new potatoes
2 cups chicken stock
7 fl oz lemon juice
salt and pepper
7 fl oz heavy cream
4 large chicken breasts
chopped fresh parsley

Peel the celeriac and carrots. Cut all the vegetables into very fine (julienne) strips and cook in separate saucepans of salted boiling water for 2–3 minutes. Drain and refresh under cold running water. Cook the potatoes until just tender and set aside with the vegetables.

Put the chicken stock in a saucepan with the lemon juice, salt, and quite a lot of pepper to "lift" the sauce. Bring to a boil, then add the cream. Cut each chicken breast into three equal pieces and add to the creamy chicken stock. Simmer gently for 8–10 minutes or until cooked through.

Add the cooked potatoes and vegetable strips and cook for a further 2–3 minutes. Serve in soup plates, sprinkled with chopped parsley.

Waterzooi de homard (Lobster and Mussels with Vegetables)

SERVES 2

¾ cup carrots

¾ cup celeriac

¾ cup trimmed leeks

6 new potatoes

1 whole lobster (about 1 lb 2 oz), cooked

7 fl oz lobster bisque (see page 31)

10 mussels, well scrubbed

chopped parsley

Peel the carrots and celeriac. Cut all the vegetables into very fine (julienne) strips and cook in separate saucepans of salted boiling water for 2–3 minutes. Drain and refresh under cold running water. Cook the potatoes until just tender and set aside with the vegetables.

Cut the lobster lengthwise and then in half, separating the body and claws from the tail.

Put the lobster bisque in a wide saucepan to heat through. Add the lobster and mussels and simmer for 5 minutes. Add the potatoes and vegetables and simmer for a further 2 minutes.

To serve, divide the lobster and mussels between two soup plates, pour the sauce over the top, and sprinkle with chopped parsley.

Bloedpans au vinaigre de xérès (Blood sausage with sherry vinegar)

SERVES 2
2 apples
½ cup brown sugar
½ cup butter
¾ lb blood sausage (black pudding)
2 tablespoons sherry vinegar
salt and pepper

Peel and halve the apples and remove the cores. Cut each half into three pieces and toss in the brown sugar. Melt a tablespoon of the butter in a skillet, add the apple pieces, and cook over low heat until they are tender and brown. Remove from the pan and keep warm.

Cut the blood sausage into 12 slices and fry in the same pan for 4 minutes. Arrange the apple slices in a fan or ring shape on two warmed plates. Remove the blood sausage from the pan and put on the plates with the apple.

Add the sherry vinegar to the skillet, and cook, stirring, for 1 minute. Whisk the remaining butter into the pan to complete the sauce. Season to taste, then pour the sauce over the apples and blood sausage and serve hot.

Stoemp saucisse (Belgian sausages and mashed potatoes)

SERVES 4
4–6 potatoes, peeled
4 tablespoons butter
1 carrot, diced
1 leek, chopped
¼ head of Savoy cabbage, shredded
12 good pork or wild boar sausages
½ cup heavy cream
salt and pepper
freshly grated nutmeg

Boil the potatoes until tender, drain, and mash.

Melt half the butter in a saucepan, add the carrot, cover, and cook over very low heat for 5–10 minutes. Add the leek and cabbage and continue to cook until all the vegetables are tender.

Meanwhile, broil or fry the sausages until cooked through.

To serve, reheat the mashed potato. Beat in the remaining butter and the cream. Season to taste with salt, pepper, and nutmeg, and stir in the vegetables. Serve hot, surrounded by the sausages.

Pâte sucrée
(Sweet pie crust)

MAKES A 10-inch PIE CRUST

1¾ cups all-purpose flour

½ cup sugar

½ cup butter, softened

1 egg yolk

Preheat the oven to 350° F.

    Sift the flour into a bowl and stir in the sugar. Add the butter and egg yolk, and mix lightly with your fingertips until the mixture forms coarse crumbs. Add about 1 tablespoon ice-cold water and mix lightly to form a dough. Wrap the dough and let rest in the refrigerator for 20–30 minutes.

    Roll out the dough to about ¼-inch thick and use to line a 10-inch tart pan. Cover the crust with tin foil and fill with baking beans. Bake in the oven for 10 minutes, then remove the tin foil and beans, and bake for a further 5 minutes. Remove from the oven and let cool slightly.

Tarte au citron
(Lemon tart)

SERVES 6

½ cup freshly squeezed lemon juice

grated zest of 3 lemons

1½ cups sugar

7 eggs

1 cup heavy cream

1 cooked pie crust (see above)

Preheat the oven to 250° F.

    Mix together the lemon juice and zest, sugar, eggs, and cream. Pour the mixture into the pie crust and bake for about 15–20 minutes or until firm. Let cool, then chill in the refrigerator until ready to serve.

Tarte au sucre
(Almond cream tart)

SERVES 4–6

1 cup plus 3 tablespoons sugar

½ cup ground almonds

1 cooked pie crust (see left)

3 eggs

7 fl oz crème fraîche

½ teaspoon vanilla extract

¼ cup butter

½ cup confectioner's sugar

Preheat the oven to 350° F.

    Mix the sugar with the ground almonds and spread evenly in the pie crust.

    Beat together the eggs, crème fraîche, and vanilla extract, and pour into the pie crust. Cover with tiny knobs of butter and bake for about 30 minutes or until the filling is firm. Let cool. To serve, sift the confectioner's sugar over the tart.

Tarte au riz
(Creamy rice tart)

SERVES 4–6

1 cup long-grain rice

1 heavy cream

2½ cups milk

¾ cup sugar

½ teaspoon vanilla extract

1 cooked pie crust (see above)

Put the rice, cream, milk, sugar and vanilla extract in a saucepan and simmer gently for about 1 hour, stirring frequently.

    Preheat the oven to 350° F.

    When the rice has absorbed all the liquid, pour into the pie crust and bake for 10 minutes. Let cool before serving.

BELGO'S TOP 10 FILMS TO WATCH

1. **THE SEXUAL LIFE OF THE BELGIANS**
2. **TOTO LE HERO**
3. **DAËNS**
4. **MAN BITES DOG** (*after dinner only*)
5. **TINTIN SUR LA LUNE**
6. **IF IT'S A TUESDAY IT MUST BE BELGIUM**
7. **BABETTE'S FEAST**
8. **LA GRANDE BOUFFE**
9. **UN HOMME ET UNE FEMME**
10. **WITHNAIL AND I**

Mousse au chocolat belge
(Belgian chocolate mousse)

SERVES 4
5 oz chocolate (dark, milk or white)
2 eggs, separated
2 tablespoons sugar
1 cup whipping or heavy cream

Cut the chocolate into small pieces and put in a bowl over a small saucepan of very hot water. Stir until melted and smooth, then let cool.

Mix the egg yolks with half the sugar. Whip the cream until it starts to thicken, but is not stiff.

Whip the egg whites with the remaining sugar until stiff, then gently fold into the cream. Gradually add the egg yolk and sugar mixture, then finally fold in the melted chocolate. Spoon into ramekins and let set for 4 hours before serving.

Café liegeois
(Coffee ice cream
with whipped cream)

SERVES 1
3½ fl oz whipping or heavy cream
¼ cup confectioner's sugar
1 shot of espresso
3½ fl oz milk
3 scoops of mocha ice cream

Whip the cream until it starts to thicken, then add the confectioner's sugar and whip until firm.

Mix half the coffee with the milk. Put the ice cream in a glass or bowl, add the coffee-milk mixture, and top with the whipped cream. Pour the remaining espresso over the top and serve at once.

Belgo specialties

ONCE WE FELT SATISFIED that Belgo had successfully introduced the wonderful simplicity of Belgian traditional cooking to England, we could not help being compelled to create our own signature dishes. We did this by using traditional methods or ingredients and giving them something of a modern twist.

Being in Britain gave us an opportunity to do this without having to worry too much about a Belgian public outcry for not using the beef drippings or tons of butter that some of the original recipes required. What we set out to do was to introduce a series of new dishes that would pay tribute to the ingredients and methods of the classic Belgian repertoire.

INSPECT A POIREAUX

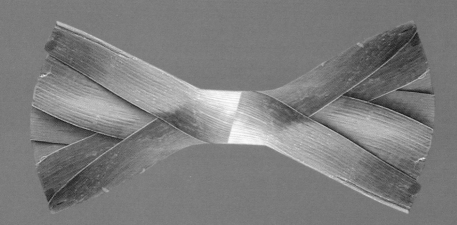

ASPARAGUS

Asperges (Asparagus)

We are often asked, "What will Belgo do if one day all the mussels in the world vanish?" Denis and André's response: "Let them eat asparagus!" So you think we lost our heads? We did that a long time ago. Quite seriously, most restaurants in Belgium, and also in the Netherlands and Germany, that have mainly mussels on their menu throughout the year, usually replace them with a selection of asparagus when seasonal supplies of mussels diminish. It just so happens that the asparagus season in northern Europe starts as the mussels enter their spawning period.

Delicious white asparagus from Malines (Mechelen) in northern Belgium is renowned for its superb texture and juiciness. Green asparagus, from the Netherlands and other parts of Belgium, is more readily available and not so expensive as the white "Malines."

Asparagus was introduced to Belgium during the period of Spanish rule and soon became a leading member of the Belgian culinary repertoire. We at Belgo make a point of celebrating asparagus all year round by giving it its own section on our menu.

SERVES 1
8 asparagus spears
salt

Trim the bottom of the asparagus and peel about halfway up the stalks.

Cook in a wide pan of boiling salted water and boil until just tender, 5–10 minutes, depending on size. Refresh under cold running water to set the green color. Pat dry and chill until needed.

LET THEM EAT ASPARAGUS!

Asperges flamande
(Warm asparagus with butter and chopped eggs)

SERVES 2
16 cooked asparagus spears
½ cup butter
1 hard-boiled egg, finely chopped
salt and pepper
juice of ½ lemon
1 teaspoon chopped fresh parsley

Put the asparagus in a pan of boiling water to heat through for 1–2 minutes. Drain, pat dry, and arrange on two warmed serving plates.

Heat the butter in a skillet until it is light brown, add the chopped egg, and salt and pepper. Cook for 45 seconds, then add the lemon juice, and pour over the warm asparagus. Sprinkle with parsley and serve at once.

Asperges meunière
(Warm asparagus with butter, lemon juice, and parsley)

SERVES 1
8 cooked asparagus spears
¼ cup butter
juice of ½ lemon
1 teaspoon chopped fresh parsley
salt and pepper

Place the asparagus in a pan of boiling water to heat through for 1–2 minutes. Drain, pat dry, and arrange on a warmed serving plate. Brown the butter in a skillet and add the lemon juice, parsley, and seasoning. Pour over the warm asparagus and serve at once.

Asperges hollandaise
(Warm asparagus with hollandaise sauce)

SERVES 2

½ cup butter

2 egg yolks

2 tablespoons white wine

juice of ½ lemon

salt and pepper

16 cooked asparagus spears

First, clarify the butter by heating slowly in a saucepan and cooking gently for a few minutes. Let cool until tepid. Using a spoon, carefully skim the impurities off the top of the butter and pour the clarified butter into a small ramekin, taking care to leave behind the impurities at the bottom of the pan.

To make the hollandaise, first heat a saucepan of water. Put the egg yolks and wine in a round-bottomed bowl, mix well, then put the bowl over the saucepan of hot water and whisk until the mixture thickens; this will take about 3 minutes.

Remove the bowl from the heat and very gradually whisk in the clarified butter. Finally add the lemon juice and salt and pepper.

Place the asparagus in a pan of boiling water to heat through for 1–2 minutes. Drain, pat dry, and arrange on two warmed serving plates. Pour the hollandaise over and serve at once.

Asperges vinaigrette
(Chilled asparagus with vinaigrette dressing)

SERVES 4

½ teaspoon Dijon mustard

½ teaspoon finely chopped shallots

½ teaspoon finely chopped garlic

½ teaspoon chopped fresh thyme

¼ cup red wine vinegar

salt and pepper

7 fl oz vegetable oil

¼ cup olive oil

32 cooked, chilled asparagus spears

Put the mustard, shallots, garlic, thyme, vinegar, and seasoning in a bowl and whisk well. Mix the two oils together and incorporate them slowly into the mixture, whisking all the time.

Divide the asparagus spears between four serving plates and either pour the vinaigrette over them or serve it separately.

Asperges ardennaise (Chilled asparagus with Ardennes ham)

SERVES 4

½ teaspoon Dijon mustard

½ teaspoon finely chopped shallots

½ teaspoon finely chopped garlic

½ teaspoon chopped fresh thyme

¼ cup red wine vinegar

salt and pepper

7 fl oz vegetable oil

¼ cup olive oil

32 cooked, chilled asparagus spears

8 slices of Ardennes ham or prosciutto

Put the mustard, shallots, garlic, thyme, vinegar, and seasoning in a bowl and whisk well. Mix the two oils together and incorporate them slowly into the mixture, whisking all the time.

Divide the asparagus spears between four serving plates and either pour the vinaigrette over them or serve it separately.

Arrange 2 slices of Ardennes ham or prosciutto on each plate.

Asperges crevettes grises (Chilled asparagus with brown shrimps)

SERVES 4

½ teaspoon Dijon mustard

½ teaspoon finely chopped shallots

½ teaspoon finely chopped garlic

½ teaspoon chopped fresh thyme

¼ cup red wine vinegar

salt and pepper

7 fl oz vegetable oil

¼ cup olive oil

32 cooked, chilled asparagus spears

¾ lb peeled brown (Gulf pink) shrimp

4 teaspoons chopped fresh chives

Put the mustard, shallots, garlic, thyme, vinegar, and seasoning in a bowl and whisk well. Mix the two oils together and incorporate them slowly into the mixture, whisking all the time.

Arrange the asparagus on the serving plates. Mix the shrimp with the chives, scatter the shrimp over the top, and pour on the vinaigrette.

LEEKS

Poireaux
(Leeks)

Leeks are tremendously versatile, delicious, and cheap. They are also a great alternative to the more expensive and seasonal asparagus. They are hugely popular in Belgium and are used throughout the cooking repertoire, braised in butter, steamed, or broiled. Leeks are just as popular in other northern European countries, such as the Netherlands and Germany.

For those of you who may not know this, the French word for leeks is *poireaux*.

So, when we introduced leeks to the Belgo menu, we could hardly resist using our poor sense of humor and naming the section Poirot's poireaux!

SERVES 1
2 lbs leeks
1 teaspoon salt
juice of ½ lemon
salt and pepper

Bring a saucepan of water to a boil. Peel off the outer leaves of the leeks and trim the root end and the top green parts, so they are all of equal length. Wash them thoroughly.

Add the salt to the boiling water, then add the leeks, and boil until they are tender right through when tested with the point of a sharp knife; this will take approximately 20 minutes, depending on size.

Mix the lemon juice with the salt and pepper and set aside.

Refresh the leeks under cold running water, then gently squeeze them dry.

Put in a shallow dish, pour over the lemon juice, and chill in the refrigerator.

They are now ready for the following recipes.

Poireaux vinaigrette
(Leeks with vinaigrette dressing)

¼ teaspoon Dijon mustard

½ garlic clove, finely chopped

½ teaspoon finely chopped shallot

good pinch of fresh thyme leaves, chopped

1 tablespoon red wine vinegar

salt and pepper

3 tablespoons sunflower oil

1 tablespoon olive oil

2 lbs cooked, chilled leeks

To make the vinaigrette, mix the mustard, garlic, shallot, thyme, vinegar, and seasoning together in a small bowl. Whisk in the oils.

Simply pour the vinaigrette over the leeks and serve.

Poireaux ardennaise
(Leeks with Ardennes ham)

Follow the recipe for poireaux vinaigrette and arrange 2 slices of Ardennes ham or prosciutto on top.

Poireaux crevettes grises
(Leeks with brown shrimp)

Follow the recipe for poireaux vinaigrette. Mix ¼ lb peeled brown (Gulf pink) shrimp with 1 teaspoon chopped fresh chives, and scatter over the leeks.

LOBSTER

Homard à l'espagnole (Lobster with garlic and olive oil)

On one of our early visits back to Belgium, while we were setting up Belgo, we met an old friend whose child was playing with the most unusual toy. It was the bottom half of a remote-controlled miniature sports car wearing the carcass of a freshly eaten lobster. He proceeded to race this "lobster" wherever we went: Supermarkets, warehouse stores, etc. He introduced his "pet" as "Homard Sharif"(*homard* being French for lobster). Quite what that little story has to do with explaining the popularity of lobsters in Belgium and on the Belgo menu we cannot answer, but we felt obliged to write it.

One thing that is for sure, though, is that lobster, *homard* in French or *kreeft* in Flemish, has an important place in the Belgian appetite. On the Place Sainte Catherine, where most of Brussels' seafood brokers and wholesalers are located, you will find five or six restaurants dedicating their menus entirely to the worship of this crustacean. Au Rugbyman restaurant celebrates the lobster in over 20 recipes. At Belgo in England, we sell some 200 lobsters a week, served in four or five different ways. Here is one of the simplest. Salut Homard!

SERVES 1–2
1 live lobster (about 1 lb 2 oz)
2 garlic cloves
3½ fl oz extra virgin olive oil
chopped fresh parsley

Preheat the broiler. Using a heavy cleaver, chop the lobster in half lengthwise. Peel the garlic and crush under the blade of the cleaver. Mix the garlic and olive oil together, then pour over the lobster. Cook the lobster under the hot broiler for about 8–10 minutes, until the flesh is just cooked and hot through. Sprinkle with parsley and serve at once, with half a lemon and salad leaves.

Omar who?

Soupe de moules
(Mussel, cream, and saffron soup)

SERVES 4

2½ lbs mussels, cleaned (see page 21)

3½ cups dry white wine

¼ cup butter

1 onion, chopped

2 celery stalks, chopped

4 leeks, chopped

generous pinch of saffron strands,
    infused in 2 tablespoons boiling water

1 cup heavy cream

beurre manié (1 tablespoon softened butter mashed with
    1 tablepoon all-purpose flour until smooth)

julienne of vegetables (2 carrots and 1 leek, cut into very fine
    strips, blanched in boiling water and refreshed in cold water)

Put the mussels in a casserole dish with the wine, over high heat, and bring to a boil. Cook until the mussels have opened, stirring frequently to ensure they are evenly cooked; this takes only a few minutes.

Strain the cooking liquid through a fine strainer into a pitcher, leaving behind any grit. Add water to make up to 3½ cups.

Discard any mussels that have not opened and remove the rest from their shells, discarding the shells.

Melt the butter in a large saucepan, add the chopped vegetables, and cook over low heat for 5 minutes, until softened but not browned. Reserve 20–30 mussels and add the rest to the vegetables, together with the strained cooking liquid; simmer for about 1 hour.

Blend the soup in a blender and pass it through a conical strainer into the cleaned pan. Add the saffron and cream, and reheat, whisking in the beurre manié to thicken the soup. Serve hot in soup plates, with the julienne of vegetables and 5–6 of the reserved mussels in each plate.

Sᴛ Jᴀᴄǫᴜᴇs ᴀᴜx ᴇɴᴅɪᴠᴇs
(Sᴄᴀʟʟᴏᴘs ᴡɪᴛʜ ʙʀᴀɪsᴇᴅ ᴇɴᴅɪᴠᴇs)

SERVES 1

5 white fish bones

2 medium onions, chopped

1 celery stalk, chopped

bouquet garni made with bay leaf, black peppercorns,
    coriander seed and fennel seed

2 tablespoons grape seed oil

4 large scallops

3 tablespoon butter

1 head of Belgian endive

1 teaspoon Demerara sugar

1 tablespoon minced shallots

pinch of blanched lime zest

6 tablespoons lemon genever

3 tablespoons lime juice

pinch of chopped cilantro

Put the fish bones, onion, celery and bouquet garni in a saucepan with 1 cup of water. Bring to a boil, then reduce the heat, and simmer for 45 minutes. Strain then season to taste.

Heat the oil in a small skillet. When hot, gently add the scallops. Cook for 3 minutes on each side or until golden brown. Remove from the skillet and set aside.

Melt 1 tablespoon of the butter in a saucepan, add the endive, and braise until brown all over. Add 2 tablespoons of water and the sugar, stirring so the sugar dissolves and caramelizes on the endive. Remove the endive from the pan, cut in half lengthwise, and arrange on a plate, cut side up.

Re-heat the skillet used for the scallops, add the shallots, and cook over low heat until translucent. Add the lime zest and the genever. Simmer until reduced by half, then add lime juice and 3 tablespoons of the fish stock and bring to a boil. Remove from the heat and stir in 1 tablespoon of the butter and the cilantro. Put the scallops on top of the endive and pour the sauce over them.

Fᴇᴜɪʟʟᴇᴛᴇ́ ᴅᴇ ᴍᴏᴜʟᴇs sᴀfʀᴀɴᴇ́
(Mᴜssᴇʟs ᴀɴᴅ sᴀᴍᴘʜɪʀᴇ
ɪɴ ᴘᴜff ᴘᴀsᴛʀʏ)

SERVES 4

½ lb puff pastry

7 fl oz heavy cream

1 teaspoon chopped shallots

generous pinch of saffron strands

1 lb cooked, shelled mussels (see left)

salt and pepper

1 lb fresh samphire

Preheat the oven to 425° F.

Roll out the puff pastry to just under ¼-inch thick and cut out four squares. Put on a dampened baking sheet and bake for 8–10 minutes or until deep golden brown. Transfer to a wire rack and let cool.

Put the cream, shallots, and saffron in a saucepan, add the mussels and a touch of seasoning, and heat gently.

Cook the samphire in boiling water for 2 minutes. Drain well.

Slice the pastry squares through the middle and arrange the bottoms on four serving plates. Pour the mussels and their sauce over the pastry bottoms and put the samphire on top. Half cover with the pastry tops and serve at once.

Escargots Ixelles
(Snail and mushroom tartlets)

SERVES 4

½ lb puff pastry

4–6 heads of Belgian endive

peanut or groundnut oil for deep frying

¼ cup butter

2 cloves garlic, crushed

24 snails

1 cup mixed mushrooms, sliced

3½ fl oz dry white wine

1 tablespoon sherry vinegar

Preheat the oven to 425° F.

Roll out the puff pastry to just under ¼-inch thick and cut out four squares. Put on a dampened baking sheet and bake for 8–10 minutes or until deep golden brown. Transfer to a wire rack and let cool.

Cut the Belgian endive in half lengthwise and cut out the cores. Slice the Belgian endive very thinly. Heat the oil for deep frying, add the Belgian endive, and sauté for 1 minute. Remove from the pan and drain for 5 minutes.

Just before serving, reheat the oil and deep-fry the Belgian endive again until it is well browned.

Melt the butter in a skillet and add the garlic, snails, and mushrooms. Sauté for 5 minutes, then add the wine and vinegar, and cook for 2 minutes.

Slice the pastry squares through the middle and arrange the bottoms on four serving plates. Spoon the snail mixture over the pastry bottoms and put the deep fried Belgian endive on top. Half cover with the pastry tops and serve at once.

Salade de Herve piquante
(Belgian cheese salad)

SERVES 2

4 Little Gem or butterhead lettuce

2 tablespoons finely chopped chives

3 tablespoons olive oil

1 tablespoon lemon juice

2 Golden Delicious apples

½ lb Herve piquante cheese

Rinse the lettuce and shred about half of it, reserving 20–25 attractive leaves. Put the chives in a bowl with the olive oil and lemon juice and mix well.

Peel and core the apples and cut into cubes. Cut the cheese into similar-sized cubes.

Mix the shredded lettuce with half the chive dressing. Put the reserved leaves upright around the sides of two individual salad bowls and put the shredded leaves in the center.

Toss the apples and cheese with the remaining dressing and spoon the mixture over the shredded lettuce.

Salade de pigeon
(Warm pigeon salad)

SERVES 2

2 slices of bread, crusts removed, cubed

¼ cup pine nuts

2 pigeon breasts

¼ cup butter

3 strips smoked bacon, thinly sliced

1 cup mushrooms, thinly sliced

2 tablespoons sherry vinegar

2 large handfuls of mixed lettuce leaves

VINAIGRETTE

¼ teaspoon Dijon mustard

½ garlic clove, finely chopped

½ teaspoon finely chopped shallot

good pinch of fresh thyme leaves, chopped

1 tablespoon red wine vinegar

salt and pepper

3 tablespoons sunflower oil

1 tablespoon olive oil

Preheat the oven to 400° F. Heat the broiler and broil the bread cubes until evenly browned. Broil the pine nuts until lightly browned: Do not let them burn. Set aside.

To make the vinaigrette, put all the ingredients in a screw-topped jar and shake well.

Season the pigeon breasts. Melt the butter in an ovenproof pan and add the pigeon, bacon, and mushrooms. When the pigeon is browned on both sides, put the pan in the hot oven. After 2 minutes, remove the pigeon to a warmed dish. Leave the mushrooms and bacon in the oven until cooked through, then transfer them to the dish with the pigeon. Put the pan over moderate heat, add the vinegar, and cook, stirring, for 1 minute.

Slice the pigeon. Toss the lettuce with a little vinaigrette and arrange in the center of two plates. Scatter the mushrooms and bacon around the outside. Put the sliced pigeon on the lettuce. Sprinkle with the croûtons and pine nuts; serve at once.

Choucroute forestière
(Sauerkraut with mushrooms)

SERVES 2

2 cups sauerkraut

⅓ cup butter

2 cups flat mushrooms, sliced

2 cups oyster mushrooms, sliced if large

½ cup dry white wine

10 asparagus spears

½ cup heavy cream

1 teaspoon Dijon mustard

Rinse and drain the sauerkraut. Melt the butter in a saucepan and add the mushrooms. Cook gently for 3–4 minutes, then add the sauerkraut and wine. Let cook over very low heat for 10 minutes, stirring occasionally.

Peel the asparagus and cook in salted boiling water until just tender. Drain well.

Put the cream and mustard in a small saucepan and heat gently: Do not boil.

Put the sauerkraut and mushroom mixture in the center of two warmed serving dishes. Pour the cream sauce around it and arrange the asparagus on the sauce. Serve at once.

Dorade à la crème de céleri (Red snapper with creamed celeriac)

SERVES 2

1 teaspoon tomato paste

1 cup tomato concassée

1 teaspoon fresh ginger, grated

¼ teaspoon cider vinegar

pinch of cayenne pepper

salt and pepper

2 bunches chervil

½ cup olive oil

1 celeriac (celery root) cut into julienne strips

1 cup heavy cream

½ lb fresh spinach

2 x ½ lb red snapper fillets

First make the tomato chutney. Put the tomato paste into a small saucepan over low heat and stir with a wooden spoon until the oil separates from the paste. Add the concassée, ginger, vinegar, cayenne pepper and season, then cook, uncovered, until all the liquid has evaporated.

Put the chervil in a pot of rapidly boiling water for not more than five seconds, then immediately plunge into ice water. Squeeze out all excess water then put in a blender with the oil and purée until smooth. Strain through cheesecloth and reserve.

Put the celeriac in a saucepan with the cream and cook over low heat until the celery root is tender.

Heat 2 tablespoons of the chervil oil in a skillet, then add in the fish, skin side down, and cook for 4 minutes or until golden brown. Turn and cook the other side until golden brown.

Steam the spinach for three to four minutes.

Make layers on each plate beginning with ¼ cup of the creamed celeriac, then pile half the spinach on top of that, followed by a fish fillet, and a dollop of tomato chutney. Drizzle chervil oil around the rim of the plate.

Saumon à la Hoegaarden (Salmon with wheat beer sauce)

SERVES 4

1¾ cups fish stock

7 fl oz crème fraîche

beurre manié (1 tablespoon butter mashed with 1 tablespoon flour)

7 fl oz Hoegaarden white beer

¼ cup pistachio nuts, finely chopped

4 pieces of salmon fillet, about ½ lb each

a little flour, for dusting the fish

oil and butter, for frying

CARAMELIZED BELGIAN ENDIVE

4 heads of Belgian endive

1 teaspoon sugar

generous pinch of nutmeg

salt and pepper

To make the caramelized Belgian endive, cut the Belgian endive into thin slices and place in a heavy-bottomed saucepan with the sugar, nutmeg, salt, pepper, and 2 tablespoons water. Cook over high heat, stirring frequently, until the Belgian endive begins to brown, then gradually reduce the heat, stirring from time to time until the Belgian endive is evenly browned and tender.

Meanwhile, boil the fish stock over high heat to reduce the liquid by half. Add the cream and boil to reduce slightly, then whisk in the beurre manié to thicken the sauce, and add the beer and pistachio nuts. Lightly dust the salmon with flour, then sauté the fillets in oil and butter. Divide the caramelized Belgian endive between four warmed serving plates. Place the salmon on the Belgian endive and pour the sauce around the fish. Serve with snow peas and boiled potatoes.

Sole à la zeebrugeoise
(Sole with lobster sauce)

SERVES 4

1¼ cups dry white wine

1 bouquet garni (celery, leek, thyme, black peppercorns, bay leaf, parsley)

1 carrot, sliced

1 small onion, sliced

4 Dover sole fillets, about 6 oz each

20 mussels, cleaned

¼ cup lobster bisque (see page 31)

5 oz peeled brown (Gulf pink) shrimp

3 new potatoes, boiled

Put the wine in a saucepan with the bouquet garni, carrot, onion, and ½ cup water, bring to a boil, and then reduce the heat to a simmer. Roll up the sole fillets and hold in place with a toothpick. Put them in the simmering liquid, add the mussels, and poach slowly for 6–8 minutes.

Meanwhile, heat the lobster bisque in a saucepan, then add the shrimp and heat through gently.

Drain the sole fillets, remove the toothpicks, and arrange on four warmed plates. Pour the lobster sauce over the sole and arrange the potatoes and mussels around the side. Serve at once.

Turbot, sauce nero
(Turbot with black sauce)

SERVES 4

2 lb spinach

2–3 sprigs of thyme

2 bay leaves

10 black peppercorns

2 shallots, sliced

4 turbot fillets, about 6 oz each

7 fl oz heavy cream

beurre manié (1 tablespoon butter mashed with 1 tablespoon flour)

7 fl oz Hoegaarden white beer

4–6 heads of Belgian endive

peanut or groundnut oil for deep frying

2 tablespoons of squid ink

salt and pepper

½ cup butter

Cook the spinach in a saucepan of salted boiling water for 1 minute. Drain, refresh under cold running water, then squeeze out all the moisture. Set aside.

Put the thyme, bay leaves, peppercorns, and shallots in a wide saucepan with 2 cups water. Bring slowly to a boil and simmer for 15 minutes, then add the turbot, and poach gently for 5 minutes. Lift out the fish and set aside, covered, in a warm place. Strain the liquid into a measuring pitcher.

Pour 1¼ cups of the liquid into a saucepan and boil over high heat to reduce the liquid by half. Add the cream and boil to reduce slightly, then whisk in the beurre manié to thicken the sauce, and add the beer. Set aside.

Cut the Belgian endive in half lengthwise and cut out the cores. Slice the endive thinly. Heat the oil for deep frying, add the endive, and sauté until golden and crisp. Drain on paper towels.

Reheat the fish cream sauce over low heat and whisk in the squid ink. Season to taste. Reheat the spinach in the butter. Put the spinach in the center of four warmed serving plates and arrange the turbot fillets on top. Pour the sauce around the spinach. Scatter the deep-fried endive over the fish and serve.

Ragoût de champignons à la Trappiste
(Mushrooms stewed in Orval beer, in a pie crust with Orval cheese)

SERVES 4

⅓ cup butter

2 onions, thinly sliced

3 cups flat mushrooms, thickly sliced

3 cups oyster mushrooms, sliced if large

7 fl oz Orval beer

1 cup heavy cream

salt and pepper

¾ lb puff pastry

8 slices of Orval cheese

Preheat the oven to 425° F.

Melt the butter in a large saucepan, add the onions, and cook over low heat for 5 minutes or until softened but not browned. Add the mushrooms and cook slowly for another 5 minutes, then add the beer, cream, and seasoning and simmer for 20–25 minutes.

Roll out the puff pastry to just under ¼-inch thick and cut out four large squares. Put on a dampened baking sheet and bake for 10 minutes or until deep golden brown. Transfer to a wire rack for a few minutes.

Slice the pastry squares through the middle and arrange the bottoms on four heatproof serving dishes. Divide the mushroom mixture between the pastry bottoms and put two slices of cheese on each. Cook under a hot broiler for 5 seconds. Replace the pastry tops and serve at once.

Salade de betteraves et chèvre (Roast beets and goat's cheese salad)

SERVES 2

10 oz goat's cheese

5 oz cream cheese

1 egg

2 tablespoons cornstarch

⅔ cup sour cream

2 tablespoons butter

2 tablespoons brown sugar

1 cup whole pecans

3 teaspoons paprika

1 teaspoon coarse salt

1 teaspoon cumin

1 teaspoon garlic powder

1 teaspoon cayenne pepper

1 teaspoon white pepper

¼ cup lambic Framboise beer

1½ fl oz tarragon vinegar

¼ cup walnut oil

¼ cup olive oil

2 tablespoons minced shallot

1 tablespoon Dijon mustard

pinch of fresh tarragon, chopped

6 arugula leaves, washed and dried

1 pear, cut into lengthwise slices and broiled until just browned

½ lb beets, sliced, broiled until just browned, and chopped

salt and pepper

Preheat the oven to 275°F. Butter and flour two ceramic ramekins.

Blend together the goat's cheese and cream cheese until creamy and smooth. Add the egg and cornstarch, season to taste, then blend again until smooth. Add the sour cream and blend once more until smooth.

Use the mixture to fill the ramekins almost to the top. Tap down to realse any air bubbles, then put in a deep ovenproof tray and add water until halfway up the sides of the ramekins.

Bake for 1½ hours or until a toothpick inserted in the center comes out clean.

Melt the butter in a saucepan. Add the brown sugar, mix until dissolved, then toss in the pecans and stir until coated with the mixture. In a medium bowl, mix together the paprika, coarse salt, cumin, garlic powder, cayenne pepper, and white pepper. While the pecans are still warm toss them in the spice mixture, then spread out on a plate and allow to cool. Once cool, chop.

In a medium bowl mix the beer, shallots, mustard, vinegar and tarragon, and season to taste. Then add the walnut and olive oils and whisk until well blended.

If necessary, warm the goat's cheese quiches in a microwave for 5–10 seconds, then remove from the ramekins.

Arrange the arugula leaves on two plates. In the center of each plate place one slice of broiled pear, then top with a quiche. Toss the chopped roasted beets in the vinaigrette and then arrange in three piles around the arugula leaves. Pour the remaining vinaigrette around the plate and over the arugula, then top the quiche with the candied pecans.

Crêpes

MAKES 4–6 CREPES

1 egg

½ cup sugar

¼ cup all-purpose flour, sifted

pinch of salt

2 tablespoons butter, melted

½ teaspoon vanilla extract

½ cup milk

2 tablespoons butter for frying

Mix together the egg, sugar, flour, salt, melted butter, and vanilla extract. Gradually pour in the milk, whisking constantly. Let mixture rest for 20 minutes.

Heat a knob of butter in a skillet over medium-high heat. Pour in a ladleful of the crêpe batter and quickly tilt the pan so the batter just covers the bottom of the pan; it must not be too thick. Let it cook for about 2 minutes, then flip it over, and cook the other side for 1 minute.

Repeat with the remaining batter, stacking the cooked crêpes on a warmed plate.

Crêpe flamande (Crêpe with caramelized apples and prunes, vanilla ice cream, and white chocolate sauce)

SERVES 1

1 apple

¼ cup butter

5–6 canned prunes, drained, pits removed

¼ cup sugar

2 oz white chocolate, chopped

3 fl oz milk

1 crêpe (see left)

2 scoops of real vanilla ice cream

Peel and core the apple and cut it into quarters. Melt the butter in a saucepan, add the apple pieces, and cook gently for 2 minutes. Add the prunes and the sugar, cover the pan with a lid, and cook for a further 5 minutes.

Into a small saucepan break the chocolate and add the milk. Heat gently, whisking constantly. When hot and thick, remove from the heat and set aside.

Place the crêpe on a warmed serving plate. Put the ice cream, apples, and prunes on the crêpe and fold over. Pour the white chocolate sauce around the pancake and serve at once.

Crêpe Belgo
(Crêpe with vanilla ice cream, mixed berries, and white chocolate sauce)

SERVES 1
2 oz white chocolate
3 fl oz milk
1 crêpe (see left)
2 scoops of real vanilla ice cream
½ cup mixed berries (raspberries, strawberries, blueberries, blackcurrants)

Into a small saucepan break the chocolate and add the milk. Heat gently, whisking constantly. When hot and thick, remove from the heat and set aside.

Put the crêpe on a warmed serving plate. Put the ice cream and berries on the crêpe and fold over. Pour the white chocolate sauce around the crêpe and serve at once.

Gaufres Belgo
(Belgian waffles)

SERVES 4
½ cup milk
3 tablespoons butter
1 vanilla bean
1½ cups all-purpose flour
1 package active dry yeast
2 eggs, separated
1 tablespoon sugar
¼ cup white beer (e.g., Hoegaarden)
½ cup preserving sugar
2 tablespoons confectioner's sugar
white chocolate sauce and mixed berries (see Crêpe Belgo, left)

Combine the milk, butter, and vanilla bean in a saucepan and bring to a boil. Remove from the heat and whisk in the flour. Cook over low heat, stirring constantly, for 3–5 minutes. Let cool, then remove the vanilla bean.

Mix the yeast with 3 tablespoons water until evenly blended. Stir into the cooled milk mixture and let rest for 1 hour.

Beat the egg yolks into the yeast mixture. In a bowl, whisk the egg whites until firm, add the sugar and a pinch of salt, and continue whisking until stiff. Fold into the yeast mixture and let rest for a further 1 hour.

Stir the beer into the mixture. To cook the waffles, pour the mixture into a waffle iron (fill the iron about a quarter full) and sprinkle with preserving sugar. Cook until the waffle is risen and golden brown.

Serve at once, sprinkled with confectioner's sugar and accompanied by warm white chocolate sauce and mixed berries.

Tarte aux pruneaux et amandes (Prune and almond tart)

SERVES 4–6

8 eggs

1 cup plus 2 tablespoons sugar

1¼ cups all-purpose flour, sifted

½ teaspoon vanilla extract

1 cup ground almonds

1¼ cups canned prunes in syrup, drained, pits removed

½ cup confectioner's sugar

FOR THE PIE CRUST

½ cup butter

1¼ cups all-purpose flour

½ cup sugar

1 egg yolk

Preheat the oven to 350° F.

To make the pie crust, sift the flour into a bowl, and stir in the sugar. Add the butter and egg and mix lightly with your fingertips until the mixture forms coarse crumbs. Add about 1 tablespoon ice-cold water and mix lightly to form a dough. Wrap the dough and let it rest in the refrigerator for 20–30 minutes.

Roll out the dough to about ¼-inch thick and use to line a 10-inch tart pan. Cover the pie crust with tin foil and fill with baking beans. Bake in the hot oven for 10 minutes, then remove the tin foil and beans, and cook for a further 5 minutes. Remove from the oven and let cool slightly.

Mix the eggs and sugar together in a large bowl. Bring a saucepan of water to a boil, then reduce the heat a little, and put the mixing bowl over the pan. Whisk the mixture until it is warm and thick, then remove the bowl from the saucepan and continue whisking until the mixture is cooled. Gradually fold the flour, vanilla extract, and ground almonds into the mixture.

Put the prunes in the pie crust. Pour the egg mixture evenly over the prunes and bake for 10–15 minutes, or until the mixture is just firm to the touch. Dust with confectioner's sugar before serving, warm or cold.

Poires pochées à la kriek (Pears in cherry beer)

SERVES 4

4 pears

2 cups kriek / cherry beer

1 cup sugar

2 cinnamon sticks (or a good pinch of ground cinnamon)

1 cup heavy cream

4 teaspoons confectioner's sugar

4 scoops of cherry beer sorbet (see page 88)

Peel and core the pears and cut in half lengthwise. Put in a saucepan with the beer, sugar, and cinnamon. Simmer gently for about 20 minutes, until the pears are tender. Remove the pears from the liquid and let cool.

Boil the cooking liquid until it is reduced to a thick syrup, then let cool.

Whip the cream until it is thick, then beat in the confectioner's sugar.

Slice the pears thinly lengthwise, without cutting through the stalk end, then place on the serving plates and press gently into fan shapes. Pour the syrup over the pears and serve with the whipped cream and a scoop of sorbet.

Beignets aux pommes
(Apple fritters)

SERVES 4

1¼ cups all-purpose flour

7 fl oz milk

1 package active dry yeast

½ cup sugar

4 apples

¼ cup butter

pinch of ground cinnamon

vegetable oil for frying

confectioner's sugar, for dusting

Sift 1 cup of the flour into a bowl, gradually blend in the milk, add the yeast and 2 tablespoons of the sugar, and set aside.

Peel, core, and cube two of the apples. Put the cubed apples in a small saucepan with the remaining sugar, butter, and cinnamon. Add 3 tablespoons water, cover the pan, and cook over low heat for 30 minutes. Let cool.

Heat the oil in a deep-fat fryer or skillet.

Peel and core the remaining two apples and cut them into ½-inch slices. Toss the slices in the remaining flour, then dip them into the yeast batter. Using a fork, take the slices out of the batter and carefully slide them into the hot oil. When the batter is golden brown, lift the fritters onto paper towel to absorb excess oil. Keep warm while you fry the remaining fritters.

To serve, divide the apple purée and fritters between four warmed plates, dust with confectioner's sugar, and serve with cream or vanilla custard sauce.

Tour de Babel Belgo
(Belgo tower of Babel)

SERVES 4

FOR THE HAZELNUT CAKE

½ cup butter

½ cup sugar

2 eggs

6 tablespoons all-purpose flour

1 cup skinless hazelnuts, chopped

FOR THE CHOCOLATE MOUSSE

5 oz (5 squares) semi-sweet or milk chocolate

¾ cup butter

4 egg yolks

½ cup plus 1 tablespoon sugar

1¼ cup heavy cream

½ cup confectioners' sugar

⅓ cup cocoa powder

To make the mousse, melt half the chocolate and butter in a pan over low heat. Whip the egg yolks and sugar in a mixing bowl until fluffy and light. In a separate bowl, whip 9 fl oz of the heavy cream and confectioners' sugar together until stiff peaks form. Sift the cocoa powder into the butter and chocolate mixture. Fold the chocolate butter melt into the egg yolks and sugar, then fold in the whipped cream mixture until all the ingredients are evenly incorporated. Refrigerate until chilled.

To make the cake, preheat the oven to 350° F. Butter then flour an 8-inch round cake pan. In a bowl, using an electric mixer, cream together the butter and sugar for about 8 minutes. With a spatula, stir in one egg a time, making sure each one is fully incorporated. Blend in the flour and nuts. Bake for 15 minutes or until golden brown and a toothpick inserted in the middle comes out clean. Melt the rest of the chocolate and whip the rest of the cream until stiff peaks form. Slice the cake into 2 circles using the bottom of a wine glass. Put one cake circle on a plate, drizzle melted chocolate on top, then spoon on half the mousse. Repeat the layers and top with the whipped cream.

Terrine aux trois chocolats
(Triple chocolate terrine)

SERVES 8

3 oz each of dark, white, and milk chocolate

3 eggs, separated

1 envelope unflavored gelatin

3 tablespoons Mandarine Napoléon

1 cup whipping or heavy cream

Line a 4-cup terrine mold or loaf tin with plastic wrap. Melt the dark chocolate in a small bowl placed over a saucepan of very hot water. Stir until smooth, then beat in one of the egg yolks.

Soak one-third of the gelatin in cold water until soft. Drain off any excess water and dissolve the gelatin in 1 tablespoon of the heated liqueur.

Whip the egg whites until stiff. Whip one-third of the cream until it is thick but not stiff, then fold in the gelatin and liqueur. Gradually fold one-third of the whipped egg whites and the chocolate mixture into the cream mixture. Pour the mixture into the lined terrine mold and let set. Repeat the process with the white and milk chocolate. Let set for at least 4 hours, then serve in slices.

Bavarois au chocolat blanc
(White chocolate bavarois)

SERVES 4

½ envelope unflavored gelatin

8 oz white chocolate, grated

3 egg yolks

¼ cup sugar

1 cup milk

1 vanilla bean

1 cup whipping or heavy cream

Soak the gelatin in cold water until it is soft. Melt 7 oz of the chocolate in a small bowl over a saucepan of hot water.

Beat the egg yolks with the sugar in a mixing bowl. Put the milk and vanilla bean in a saucepan and bring to a boil. Remove the vanilla bean. Add the gelatin and whisk into the milk. Pour the hot milk onto the egg yolk and sugar mixture, and whisk until smooth. Let the mixture cool, then stir in the melted chocolate. Whip the cream until it is thick but not stiff, then fold gently into the chocolate mixture. Divide between four ramekins, then let set in the refrigerator for at least 3 hours.

To serve, invert each ramekin onto a plate. Grate the remaining white chocolate over the top. Serve with vanilla custard sauce and either mixed berries or orange segments.

KERANG!

GENEVER

EVERY NORTHERN EUROPEAN COUNTRY has devised a knock-out concoction of some sort to accompany their beer. The Scots and the Irish have their whiskeys, the Scandinavians their akvavits, the Germans sip on their korn, the Poles and Russians on their vodkas, and Dutch and the Belgians have their genevers or Belgian gin. This is the typical Belgian aperitif and it goes superbly with fish dishes, shellfish, and crustacea but, best of all, beer.

Since Belgo stocks a huge selection of Belgian beers, we could not resist the temptation to make our bartenders' lives even more complicated by doing the same with our genever list. We decided not to carry the usual liquor that other restaurants do, not through arrogance, but simply to remain purer to the beerhall concept: Beer and schnapps, that's it. OK, OK, and a little wine. (In Belgium, it is not uncommon for some beer bars to flatly refuse to serve anything else. We dare you to ask for a Coke or mineral water! Once, when we did, we were told, *"Enze Bier…Enze Aquarium!"*

Genever (also called jenever or peket) can be traced back to the early 17th century in what is now French Flanders. The oldest recipe though, has been traced back to 1552, when a certain Dutch chap called Philippus Hermanni wrote in his book *A Concise Book on Distilling*: "…the Aqua Juniperus is the product of distilling wine using crushed juniper berries." This method came as a result of the harsh weather conditions in the Low Countries which made wine production virtually impossible. During the 16th century beer took over and the production of *eaux,* or spirits, using not only wine but also beer, fruit wine, and cereal, became very fashionable. Several health warnings were issued about the abuse of these liquors, in particular the grain or cereal type. Some things just don't change! One needs only to look at some of the party scenes in Breughel's paintings to understand that concern.

Today, and for most of the last 300 years, genever is a product of grain distillation (rye, wheat, corn, and barley), that is predominantly flavored with juniper berries during its dilution stage. Other main ingredients include dried curaçao, orange skins, ginger, cumin, cinnamon, aniseed, licorice, and cloves.

One the most popular brands of genever is distilled by the Braeckman family, who in 1918 established the Braeckman Distillery in the Zwalm valley of the Flemish Ardennes. The mineral sources and pure water streams of the region provided an ideal setting for water mills and the Braeckman family distillery, which is renowned for its smooth genever. The Braeckmans produce a wide range of *oude graanjenever* (old genever), a grain distillate with large amounts of malt spirit, which is stored in oak casks for several years. This type carries a distinctive grain taste that is more mature in color and softer on the palate. *Oude Jenever Kikendief* (Chicken Thief Old Genever), usually sold in stoneware bottles, has a purer grain taste and should be served chilled, like vodka. The *Jonge Genever* (Young Genever) is mixed with herbs such as juniper berries and cilantro. It should be served chilled as this increases its unique aroma.

Besides Breackmans, Belgo also features Stoopke, Jonge Belfort, and a wide range of fruit genevers made by the oddly named Cockney's distillery. Fruit genevers only recently became popular—although the method of flavoring with fruit is ancient—simply because of their sweetness, easier-to-please taste, and a far more moderate alcohol content: Usually 18% to 25%, instead of the usual 40% proof. Flavors vary from the sweeter and more exotic walnut, lychee, or mandarin, to a more subtle apple or lemon.

Other speciality brands, such as Hertekamp and Peterman, are distilled by Bruggeman. The Wortegemsen Distillery, established by Albert Kint, produces a wonderful lemon pulp genever that accompanies shellfish and fish dishes quite superbly.

In London, Belgo sells over 100 bottles of genever a week.

This is why our unique, custom-made schnapps shot sticks, which can carry up to 32 chilled shots at a time, come in very handy. We also use genever in many of our traditional dishes such as *poussin à la brabançonne* and in desserts like *sorbet au geneve braeckmans au citron*. It is also very useful for marinades, especially for game and wild fowl.

A Brief
History of Belgium

OUR BOOK WOULD NOT be complete without a flash tribute to the rich historical background of the territory known to us today as: Belgium. This beloved food and beer paradise has had as many foreign rulers as Italy has had presidents in the last few years (scusa!). So, the idea of foreigners using Belgian soil to settle their disputes (does Waterloo ring a bell?), setting up a trade center (European or World H.Q.'s galore), or simply the passage to Gaule and Teutonic forests (Euro Highway Number 9 or is it 69 to Hamburg?), is nothing new to the locals who have always been too busy, getting their own state together, to notice.

P.S. DON'T MENTION WATERLOO

Mr Belgo's
HISTORICAL LOOK AT BELGIUM

HAIL CAESAR!

The first fifteen minutes of fame for Belgium came when Julius Caesar wrote: "Of all the enemies I have encountered, of all the Gauls, the Belgians were the bravest." As it happened, Caesar and his Romans stuck around in Belgae for another 500 years of pure misery.

LATINS AND SAXONS

After the Roman's left, the local "Belgian" Celts were forced to share the land with the rather unpleasant Teutonic tribes. From the very beginning, Belgium was to deal with this "two nations" problem: Celts and Teutons or Latins and Saxons, and now Flemings and Walloons.

CHARLEMAGNE WAS A BELGIAN

Europe's first great emperor, Charlemagne, was not German, not French, but Belgian (he was born on Belgian soil, in Liège, in 742). He was responsible for dividing Europe into three tribal nations. He was also semi-successful at keeping them from each other's throats. Under Charlemagne's guidance, the Belgians learned rapidly how to live between such powerful neighbors as the French and the Germans. Indeed, learning to benefit from both cultures and their riches, the Belgians quickly established themselves as serious traders.

THE FIRST BELGIAN TRADE BOOM

Between the 12th century and 16th centuries, the Low Countries were one of the richest places in the world. Early trade centers in Flanders, such as Bruges and Antwerp, were extremely powerful and commanded most of the European medieval trade market, particularly for wool and the rest of the textile industry.

HERE COME THE FRENCH

In the 15th century, with the arrival of the French Burgundian court in about 1430, Belgium flourished as an important center for the arts and architecture under the rule of Philip the Good, and later his son, Charles the Bold. Great artists such as Jan van Eyck and Rogier Van der Weyden benefited from the court's patronage.

HERE COME THE AUSTRIANS

When Charles the Bold died, his daughter Mary married Austrian Prince Maximilian I. Much to the annoyance of the French king, Mary died unexpectedly, thereafter leaving all the riches of the Lowlands to her Austrian husband. This marked the beginning of Austrian Hapsburg rule, a bit of war, and a great deal of unrest.

In the beginning…

BELGO'S TOP

10 THINGS TO DO

WHILE IN BELGIUM

1. **VISIT THE GENTSE FEESTEN** *(the beer festival in Ghent).*
2. **SHOP AT THE MAROLLEN FLEA MARKET** *in Brussels.*
3. **BAR CRAWL IN ANTWERP.**
4. **EAT AT PIERRE WYNANT'S RESTAURANT,** *comme chez soi.*
5. **VISIT THE ATOMIUM** *before they pull it down.*
6. **STUMBLE INTO THE** *Maison des Brasseurs (Brewer's House) on Grande Place.*
7. **TRY THE STEAK DE CHEVAL** *at the Brabançon restaurant in Brussels.*
8. **STAY IN THE ARDENNES** *for a few days.*
9. **JOG ON ÖOSTENDE BEACH** *while listening to Marvin Gay on your Walkman.*
10. **VISIT THE CENTER BELGE DE LA BANDE DESSIGNÉE** *Comic strip museum in Brussels.*

HERE COME THE SPANIARDS

Maximilian the Austrian was succeeded by his son Philip the Handsome. (This is not a joke.) He married a Spanish princess who gave birth to Charles V in 1500. Out went the Austrians, in came the Spanish. Charles V inherited the Kingdom of Spain *and* the Holy Roman Empire. He named Brussels as the capital of the Spanish Netherlands, and during his reign Antwerp became the most important trading city in Europe. Worn out with managing his vast territories, he retired to a monastery in 1557, leaving Austria to his brother and Spain and the Netherlands to his son.

HERE COMES THE INQUISITION

Philip II of Spain, the son of Charles V, brought in the Inquisition, which did not go down too well with the Calvinists. Most of the period from the mid-16th century to the mid-18th century was riddled with wars and social unrest. Belgium, which became part of the Austrian empire again in the early 18th century, was continuously having to deal with other people's problems: The Spanish against the French, the French against the Austrians, and so on.

BELGIUM IN DEUTSCH: NON MERCI!

One of the most important events in Belgium's history took place in 1789 in the Brabant Province, when the Brabant people revolted against Austrian Emperor Joseph II's plans to turn Belgium into a German-speaking state. The revolt was a complete success due to the people's united front against foreign domination. Ruling was one thing but converting was another. This "unity" incited the people to proclaim their territory as the land of a "united Belgium". The revolt of 1789 managed to get rid of the Austrians for a short while. The Austrians came back only to get their marching orders by Napoleon's army. Brussels and the rest of Belgium was thereafter declared French territory.

INDEPENDENCE: PART 1

The outcome of the battle of Waterloo (1815) was significant in bringing Belgium one step closer to self determination. For better or for worse, the main foreign powers led by Britain and Austria linked the State of Belgium to the Republic of Netherlands and called it the United Netherlands. Later, when William I of Orange was officially appointed king, it became known as the United Kingdom of the Netherlands.

CATHOLICS AND CALVANISTS: ALL FOR ONE?

From the start this marriage had no chance: A Catholic nation was asked to live under a Protestant's rule. The combination of Catholics and Calvinists never made a great cocktail. William I also made a serious mistake in declaring Dutch the official language of both states. Brussels being, and having been for a long time now, mainly French-speaking, was not going to accept this. (Brussels was the capital of the Belgian State and had great influence on the rest of the country.) Revolution was imminent.

REVOLUTION AT THE OPERA

On August 25, 1830, many of Brussels' most influential citizens and radicals were attending an opera by Auber called *Masianello* or *La Muette de Portici*, which carried a very strong nationalistic aria devoted to the love of the Fatherland. The words "far better to die than to live a wretched life in slavery and shame…away with the foreigners who laugh at

BELGO'S TOP 10 FAMOUS BELGIANS

1. **ANDRÉ PLISNIER SNR.**
   (Spitfire ace)
2. **JAN BUCQUOY** *(Film director: The Sexual life of the Belgians)*
3. **JACQUES BREL**
   (Singer and poet)
4. **ADOLPHE SAX**
   (Inventor of the saxophone)
5. **ENZO SCHIFFO**
   (Soccer player)
6. **BENOIT POELVOORDE**
   (Actor: Man Bites Dog)
7. **HERGÉ**
   (Tintin's creator)
8. **MANNEKEN-PIS**
   (Statuette in Brussels)
9. **JOHNNY HALLIDAY**
   (Singer)
10. **DRIES VAN NOTEN**
    (Designer)

our torment!" threw the audience into a frenzy. That was it. The place went nuts and the people of Belgium had a revolution. So much for the Beatles and the Sex Pistols, eh?

INDEPENDENCE: PART 2

Exactly one month later, on September 25, William I's Dutch troops were defeated and the people of Belgium declared themselves independent. This was made official on October 4, 1830. France, Britain, and Austria confirmed it at the London Conference on July 20, 1831, and the following day Leopold I of Saxe-Coburg, an Austrian, was proclaimed the first King of the Belgians and the independent State of Belgium. Leopold was an uncle of Queen Victoria. He had married a French woman called Louise, which pleased the French very much.

JULY 21: BELGIAN INDEPENDENCE DAY

The Belgians celebrate their independence day every year on July 21. Belgo created Belgian National Week, making this day part of a seven-day celebration of food, drink, and Belgian culture.

LEOPOLD II

Famous for his great white beard and his affair with a dancer named Chloe, the promiscuous Leopold inherited the language disputes and in-fighting between the Flemings and the Walloons that plagued his father's reign. He did manage to take a bold step toward colonization by acquiring a piece of African land fertile with coffee, sugar, cocoa, and other luxury commodities. He named it the Belgian Congo.

BELGO'S TOP 10 FUNNY NAMES OF BRUXELLEOIS RESTAURANTS

1. **PETIT BEDON**
   (Little Gut).
2. **DOUX WAZOO**
   (Soft Wazoo).
3. **IDIOT DU VILLAGE**
   (The Village Idiot).
4. **MOULES A GO GO**
   (Mussels a Go Go).
5. **O'COMME 3 POMMES**
   (Like 3 Apples).
6. **SPINNENKOPKE**
   (Spider Head).
7. **RADIS À BRETELLES**
   (Radish Suspenders).
8. **VOLEUR DE BETAIL**
   (Cattle Thief).
9. **VOLLE GAS**
   (Full Steam).
10. **IN DE KWAK**
    (In the Kwak).

BELGIUM AND THE WORLD WARS

Belgium got more territory from the Germans at the end of the First World War. Leopold II's grandson, Leopold III, had barely been proclaimed king before finding himself at war again when Belgium was invaded by Hitler's Germany. Belgium was declared "neutral," which provoked many to suspect Leopold III of collaboration with the Nazis. He never truly recovered from this accusation and later abdicated, giving his throne to his son Baudouin, aged 20.

BAUDOUIN

King Baudouin married a Spanish woman called Fabiola in 1960. His reign was marked with some controversy: The bloody withdrawal from the Congo (now Zaire) and his anti-abortion stance. These issues distanced him from his liberal-minded people. Baudouin was Belgium's longest-reigning monarch and was succeeded by his brother Albert II.

FAST FACTS ABOUT BELGIUM

1. There are ten provinces.
2. Belgium has three official languages: Flemish, French, and German.
3. The population of Belgium is 10 million (6.1 Flemish, 3.2 French, 0.7 German).
4. Brussels is the capital of the European Union and home to NATO World Headquarters.
5. Brussels has over 20,000 foreign diplomats.
6. The monetary unit is the Belgian Franc.
7. Belgium hosted the 1958 World's Fair.
8. The Atomium building was designed in 1958 by André Waterkeyn and is a complete replica of the iron molecule magnified 165 billion times.

Denis and Andrè's

TOUR OF BRUSSELS

We couldn't leave the subject of Belgium without giving you a short guided tour of our favorite restaurants, shops, people, and sites. Rain or rain, we love Brussels! Allez...

Here we are smack in the middle of the Grande-Place, one of Europe's most amazing town squares. André and Denis can never decide on which way to look first.

(Above) Potferdoome la friture est fermée.
(Below left) Nothing like a pause-café at the
art deco Palace Falstaff.
(Right) Notre "grand pei" Albert-Jean Niels,
owner of Le Canterbury.

BELGO'S TOP 10

BRUXELLEOIS RESTAURANTS

1. **AU BRABANÇON,**
   75 rue de la Commune,
   tel. 0044-2-217-7191.

2. **LA BONNE HUMEUR,**
   244 Chemin de Louvain,
   tel. 0044-2-230-7169.

3. **LE VIEUX ST. MARTIN,**
   38 Place du Grand Sablon,
   tel. 0044 -2-512-6476.

4. **LE CANTERBURY,**
   2 Avenue de l'Hippodrome,
   tel 0044-2-646-8393.

5. **SPINNENKOPKE,**
   1 Place du Jardin aux Fleurs,
   tel. 0044-2-511-8695.

6. **LE PETIT PONT,**
   114-116 rue du Du Doyennee,
   tel. 0044-2-346-4949.

7. **AUX ARMES DE BRUXELLES,**
   rue des Bouchers,
   tel. 0044-2-511-5550.

8. **CHEZ HENRI,**
   113 rue de la Flandre,
   tel. 0044-2-219-6415.

9. **CHEZ VINCENT,**
   8-10 rue des Dominicains,
   tel. 0044-2-511-2303.

10. **LE MARIE JOSEPH,**
    quai au Bois a Brules,
    tel. 0044-2-219-6415.

In the background
is the Maison des
Brasseurs on the
Grande-Place.
Check out the
brewing museum.

(Left) After some heavy-duty shopping,
stop for a beer at Le Coq. Beware: It's not for the
average tourist. (Above) Then have lobster at the
Rugbyman on Place Ste. Catherine.

The Mannekin-Pis off the Grande-Place is bound to get you going.`

(Above) A trip to the Maison Dandoy will not help your diet. For over 100 years, they have been making the best gingerbread men and speculoos and pain à la grecque. (Left) Denis and André always enjoy a good healthy selfish shellfish debate on the rue des Bouchers.

(Above) A trip to Wittamer on the Place du Grand Sablon is a must for all chocoholics. (Right) Notre "grand-mei" Marie-Jeanne Lucas from the Brabançon restaurant. (Below) Toone is the oldest string-puppet theatre in the world.

CHOCOLAT

I T IS NOT UNCOMMON for André and Denis, when at one of their favorite tables in Brussels, to pass on having dessert. This is obviously not for dietary reasons but rather for a quick detour off to Wittamer on the Place du Grand Sablon, Brussel's fashionable antique quarter, for the world's best handmade praline chocolate pastries. Established by Henri Wittamer back in 1910, Wittamer is a must for any serious gastro-tourist. Every tart, truffle, praline, and cake is handcrafted in the original restaurant premises by the Wittamer family artisans, who have steered away from the temptation of global mass production and a larger slice of the financial torte that some of their rivals have benefited from over the last decade.

One can sit on the beautiful terrace facing the Nôtre Dame du Sablon church and have delightful Belgian-style cappucino with fresh cream and sprinkled with delicious shavings of dark Wittamer tablet chocolate. This is usually how we end our work-related excursions to Brussels. What a tough job we have! On our way to La Gare du Sud (Zuid if you are Flemish) to catch our Eurostar train back to London, the assortment of fine chocolate pralines we will have bought from Wittamer for market research and development (yeah, sure, says the Belgo accountant) will have long been consumed. And speaking of consumption, the 10 million Belgians rival the British in consuming the same amount of chocolate (being 16 pounds) per head per year. We can add that the quality may differ on the British side of the channel!

True Belgian chocolate pralines are handmade from the worlds best chocolate, with a minimum of 70% cocoa solids, using fresh cream and butter with no preservative agents. Now we should clarify the meaning of the word praline, which is often misunderstood. The English recognize pralines as being any chocolate that is filled with a chocolate and nut paste. The Belgians, Germans, and the Swiss accept any high-quality fine chocolate that is filled as a genuine "praline."

Belgo uses Belgian *Callebaut* "couverture" chocolate in all its chocolate desserts.

BELGIAN CHOCOLATIER

5 STEPS

THE ART OF TASTING FINE CHOCOLATE

1. LOOK
Make sure you see a soft shine.

2. BREAK
Snap the chocolate: A good clean break indicates a fine blend.

3. SMELL
The aroma of the clean break should be one of fragrant chocolate.

4. FEEL
The texture of the chocolate against the roof of your mouth should be creamy and velvety smooth. A grainy texture indicates poor refining.

5. EXPERIENCE
Taste fine chocolate at room temperature The initial taste should be of a nutty, roasted chocolate flavor followed by a well-blended sweetness.

Stillekens
OEN

BELGO'S TOP

10 SLANG

BRUXELLEOIS

1. POTTEPEI
(silly man or drinking buddy)

2. MEI OR PEI
(pal or friend)

3. KIEKENFRETER
(chicken eater)

4. STOEFFE NEK
(poser)

5. BOLLEKE
(glass for De Koninck beer)

6. OMNUZEL
(idiot)

7. STOEMELINGS
(sneaking something)

8. POTFERDOOME
(damn, blast)

9. SMEERLAP
(bastard)

10. STILLEKENS OEN
(nice and easy does it)

OK, so this is not the greatest scenic shot from the Atomium, but heck, you've got to see it to believe it. Built in 1958 for the World's Fair.

Let's be honest, Denis and André snuck into 1st class for this shot only. Eurostar to Brussels, Brussels to Belgo, eh pei, c'est le paradis!

HOME AT LAST!

INDEX

ACKNOWLEDGMENTS

Denis and André wish to thank the following people and Spirits for making this book possible:

A giant special thanks to all our kitchen chefs team (past and present). In particular Phillipe Blaise for compiling all our recipes. Also Richard Coates, Charles Noorland, Muir Pickens, Brian Sullivan, Carlton Dennis and the rest of the kitchen crew. Also thanks to Bobby for getting us going. Nest Mertens, Albert-Jean Niels, Marie-Jeanne Lucas, Miguel and Titje for depth and knowledge on the material. Katherina Ujlaki and Mary Norman for the support, research, and great time management. John Lawrence Jones and Stephen Aland for fab food and D n' A shots. Phil Starling for Belgo shotes and Simon Wheeler for the mussles on a rope photograph. Frank "ping-pong" Schott outer sleeve shot of D n' A. Uli Sigg for styling, shooting and bass. Susan Haynes, Nick Clark, Maggie Ramsay and Laura Washburn at W&N. The Senate and Nigel Soper for graphics. John Codling for all original artowrk and logo. Michael Jackson for foreword and support, Debbie Woodcock and Meanlie Ellis press. A huge thanks to the best management team in da world: André Blais, Tim Power, Chris Burter, Tim Warner, Myriam Mavros, Danny Bjelcevic, Zoe Adjey, Craig Truter, Luigi Clerici, Suzette Tegally, André Delanchy, and Deon van Niekerk Aber, Simon. Also beg thanks to Jacky Kitching and Graeme Noble for getting Centraal through the heat. Major thanks to Richard Koch for believing in us and Sir Paul Judge for patience. Monique Van den Hurk for brilliant future designs and arhitecture and Quentin Reynolds for colors. Also Anand Zenz and Ron Arad for Noord and Centraal. Chris at the Ivy for inspiration. Meyer, Meike, Uwe, Robert, Dr Mathesius of Taschen Köln and Johnathan from Paul Smith.

Personal thanks from Denis to: my wife Danka and Egg, the best brother in the world Ptit'Dé, franek and Wisia, Tomek, Jasia, Piotr, Maman et Papa, André, Flynn, Camille, Christian "Big Bucks", Nathalie, "Mighty Max", Nadie et Alexandre, Ben Estelle and jean et Sophie, Marc and Caroline et Sebastien, Steve and Victoria et Natasha. HP for keeping me sane and André for keeping me insane and putting up with !

Personal thanks from Andr´to Ezme, my wife, for being a loving critic of my cooking; my mother, Jenny, for honing my palate with tender carbonades flamandes; my father for teaching me toeat brown shrimp without removing the heads; my step-father, Nils, for eating as many moules as me; my Belgian grandmother, Gigi, for passing on the secrets of Belgian home cooking; my niece Alice for enjoyhing Belgo moules, aged three; my sister Maryse for her delicious Soupe Verte; my brother Bobby for always staying one step ahead of the competition; my sisters Annabel and Sophie for having rawled the Brussels eateries with me; my friend and partner Denis for still being there eleven years later; and the friends who believed in Belgo; John Toosey and his Salade Liegeoise and a perfect frite; Nick Reynolds, the Brown Fairy; Richard Koch and Sir Paul Judge for putting their money where our mouths were; Mandy for teaching me office manners; Dr A Mordecai for his spiritual council; Barry McMurdoch for teaching me to take risks: Jurgen and Katherina for "another" perspective; Raynold for looking after Charlie for two years; and last but not least all the Belgo team who continue to amke it what it is now.

Text copyright © Denis Blais and André Plisnier
Color photographs copyright © 1997 Weidenfe[l] Nicolson
Day trip to Brussels pix copyright © 1997 Deni[s] and André Plisnier
Photograph p.18 copyright © 1997 Simon Whe[eler]

Published by Clarkson Potter/Publishers, New Y[ork] York. Member of the Crown Publishing Group. Random House, Inc., Toronto, London, New York Sydney, Auckland
www.randomhouse.com

Originally published in hardcover in the United Kingdom by George Weidenfeld & Nicolson Ltd i[n] Paperback edition originally published in the U[nited] Kingdom by Phoenix Illustrated, Orion Publishin[g] Group, in 1998.

CLARKSON N. POTTER, POTTER, and colophon a[re] registered trademarks of Random House, Inc.

Printed in Italy

Library of Congress Cataloging-in-Publishing D[ata] available upon request.

ISBN 0-609-80636-X

10 9 8 7 6 5 4 3 2 1

First American Edition

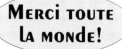

MERCI TOUTE LA MONDE!

BELGO SAYS AU REVOIR AND HOPE TO SEE YOU SOON!